GRANITE CITY

THE LIFE OF A BANDIT

I have tried to recreate events, locales and conversations from my memories of them. In order to maintain their anonymity in some instances, I have changed the names of some individuals and places. I may also have changed some identifying characteristics and details such as physical properties, occupations, and places of residence to protect the anonymity of those still living.

Although the author and publisher have made every effort to ensure that the information in this book was correct at press time, the author and publisher do not assume and hereby disclaim any liability to any party for any loss, damage, or disruption caused by errors or omissions, whether such errors or omissions result from negligence, accident, or any other cause.

Book cover design by
rehmanx_x

Edited by Leigh Jane Lyman

For my parents.

Captain Clayton Spells and Martha "Bobbie" Spells

Abandon all hope of ever having a better past.

Norman Spells

PROLOGUE

High on a hill, the red granite walls of the ominous-looking South Dakota State Penitentiary look down on the city of Sioux Falls, South Dakota. I can still remember looking at the temperature gauge on a downtown bank as my father and I drove past it on our way up that hill. The gauge read fourteen degrees, a temperature that seemed to match the chill in the car as we continued up the hill, past sparse clumps of leafless trees along the road leading to the main gate of my future home.

My journey to a prison known as Granite City had begun back in May of 1973, after a long weekend of partying and riding with my brothers in the Bandidos motorcycle club. To my way of thinking, fate has a funny way of introducing you to your destiny, and my fate began when we rumbled up to a Sioux Falls bar known as the J and M Tavern.

My world was a violent one at the time. A violent world encapsulated within a closed society that celebrated endless partying and riding and fighting.

So, it was no surprise that after a long day of doing just that, a fight broke out near closing time. Naturally, guns and knives came out and shots were fired, and in that brief, violent period of time, my fate was sealed.

But before I get into the details of my biker days beginning in chapter three, those of you who would like to know some of the reasons behind my decision to join the Bandidos should begin at the beginning.

CHAPTER 1

I have no memory of the Louisiana Delta where I was born in the waning days of WWII. My earliest memories are of the Gulf Coast of Texas after my family had moved to Flour Bluff, a low-lying spit of land near Corpus Christi that faced the shallow mud flats separating the Texas mainland from Padre Island.

Like a lot of people, I'm not actually sure if my memories of a time when I was only two years old are real or if they are images put there from looking at old black and white photographs, but it all seems real enough to me. I remember that everywhere I looked, there were tall palms and scrubby mesquite trees, famous for the wood used to flavor some of the best slow-cooked barbeque brisket in the country.

For the most part, the unpaved streets were covered with a mixture of broken oyster shells and hard caliche that turned into some form of evil Silly Putty when it rained. Texas asphalt they called it. And there were sea gulls. Lots and lots of sea gulls, their screeches filling the air.

The windows of our wood-framed house opened out from overhead hinges to let the coastal breezes through the screens. Without screens, the swarms of mosquitos would have made our lives unbearable. Almost as unbearable as the humidity we tried to chase away with the low-slung ceiling fans that spun slowly overhead.

Corpus Christ back then was a lot like New Orleans in that respect. Sultry, semi-tropical air bathed the land and the people who lived on it with thick moist air. Some folks even said you could drink it. I can't recall much of a winter.

In Flour Bluff, the well water tasted sulfurous. Out of a sense of self-preservation, my mother used to send my brother and I to the local Texaco station to draw our water from the only city water line. These were adventurous times. We played along the sandy shore and splashed our way through land-locked ponds and wetlands containing alligators, snakes and other creatures lurking in their murky waters.

For the most part, I was a happy little kid. Skinny and anemic, I ran around barefoot regardless of the sticker burrs. We lived within walking distance of the bay, and I learned to swim at an early age. We all did. To live by the coast and not know how to swim was asking for trouble, especially if you were a kid who liked to tag along with an adventurous big brother and his friends.

Back then, my father worked as a leverman on a dredge boat, a barge-like affair that sucked the mud from the mud flats to create channels for boat traffic. My father had a part in the early development of the Intercoastal Canal, an inland waterway that allowed boats to follow the East and Gulf Coast states all the way to the Mexican border at Brownsville. Out of necessity, our family followed the dredges in a nomadic lifestyle that resulted in me attending at least seven different elementary schools growing up.

Because of the constant moving, I was always the new kid and struggled with the difficulty of not being able to build lasting relationships. Without any lasting friends, I felt isolated and began to live vicariously through movies and television shows. I dreamed of living the idyllic family lifestyle of the 1950s and pictured myself living in a family like the ones I saw in "Leave It to Beaver" or "Father Knows Best".

For the most part, I lived in an isolation-induced fantasy world up until the time we finally settled down in the small coastal town of Aransas Pass, Texas, sometime in the summer of 1954. Aransas Pass at that time was famous for having the largest shrimp boat fleet in the country and maybe even the world. They celebrated this fact by holding an annual three-day festival known as the "Shrimporee", a festival that still continues to this day even though the shrimp fleet has long since moved on.

Around this time my parents became concerned that I was too skinny and took me to a doctor who diagnosed me with anemia. I began taking a series of weekly injections that eventually caused me to gain weight. To this day I believe he had the formula wrong, because I soon found myself on the other end of the weight spectrum. I became the fat kid who lived in a trailer park, and when I looked at the other kids and the cool way their Levi's fit, all I saw was the roll of fat hanging over my belt when I looked in the mirror.

My brother left for the Marines when I was only 10. For the most part, he spent the time we lived together giving me pure hell, but I remember him knocking a boy out of his chair in the park's recreation room for making fun of me. With him gone, it was left to me to help take care of our ailing mother. She suffered from a myriad of problems, including asthma and what she always referred to as "nerves". Now that my brother was gone, it was up to me to be the man of the house and to take care of Momma when my dad was away.

By the time I was twelve, I was driving her to the emergency room in the family car. I was pulled over more than once by the highway patrol for driving without a license, but they always gave me a pass. I firmly believe the police back then were more sympathetic. It's not hard to see why I didn't enjoy my childhood. Rather I endured it. I lived a great deal of my life in a fantasy world, and it's no mystery to me now as to why I love books and movies so much.

I had an uncle on my mother's side that everyone called Pot, a nickname he acquired in the 1930s after being rolled down a Mississippi River levy in an old iron washpot. Uncle Pot was a stone wino. This man was the lowest of the low when it came to being an alcoholic. He would actually hock his glasses for 50 cents to buy a half pint bottle of wine. I saw him numerous times while growing up on family trips to Louisiana. During these visits, I vividly remember smelling the urine and feces-soaked overalls he wore for days on end.

Back in those days, it seemed that there was a camaraderie among the winos in town. Whenever one of them dried up after a few months at the county penal farm, he would go to work on the river for as long as he could handle it while the others awaited his return with a paycheck they spent on wine. When all his money ran out, another one would go to the penal farm and start the cycle all over again.

Uncle Pot was a major player in this world. He was a good cook when he was sober, and he had no problem finding work on one of the many boats that traveled up and down the Mississippi River. When he could handle the sobriety no longer, he would return and donate his check to the communal wine fund.

I remember the last time I saw him before he died. I was in my early twenties and asked him for a cigarette and he told me he only had a few he bought for himself. Later, after he smoked all of his, he asked me for a cigarette from a pack I just bought. I told him, "I only have a few I bought for myself". He looked at me and said, "Gimme one and then you won't have to carry so many with you." I learned that day not to try to beat an old wino at his own game.

Living in Aransas Pass, I was finally able to cultivate some friendships. However, I soon realized that I did not have the conveniences and luxuries that most of my friends had. All of my friends were living the kind of life that I had always dreamed of living. They lived in the same house growing up, their mothers were healthy and active in

3

their community, and for the most part, their fathers were home every night.

In the early autumn of 1961, at the start of my junior year in high school, I went out for the football team. I was accepted on the junior varsity team, and for the first time in my life, I was appreciated for being bigger than the other kids and felt like an important member of the team. I was urged to hit people, which turned out to be a perfect outlet for my anger and low self-esteem, and I couldn't wait to be moved up to the varsity team the following year. Problem was, it never happened.

At the start of the next football season in 1962, our football coaches were holding the grueling "two a day" practice sessions during the dog days of summer in the blistering South Texas heat. Today, players are hydrated before, during and after practice, but the common wisdom of the day was to pump us full of salt tablets and give us only ice chips until after practice to keep us from throwing up.

Unbeknownst to me at the time, I had been born with a bad kidney, and the salt and chronic dehydration was a recipe for disaster. It wasn't long before I was physically unable to tolerate football practice anymore and I was forced to give up the first thing that had given my life meaning.

During the early part of that junior year, my grades also began to fail. Without sports and the feeling of being a member of a team, I lost the incentive to maintain my studies and started cutting school. In the middle of that year, I cut my hair in a Mohawk. When I showed up at school the next day, I was sent to the principal's office and given a three-day expulsion. After that, there were other incidents concerning my truancy and tardiness. Feeling left out and with my life spiraling out of control, I decided to quit school and go to work.

For a while, I bounced around working in various places in Aransas Pass. By now, my brother was out of the Air Force and was working on the same dredge boat with my father. I had my parents sign an emancipation document allowing me to work for the same dredging company, and a few weeks later, I was soon working with both of them in Pascagoula, Mississippi.

On a dredge boat, work goes on twenty-four hours a day. Dredges are basically huge, reconverted Mississippi River tugs outfitted with powerful diesel engines and a gigantic cutter blade that slices its way across the muddy bottom to carve out a channel. At the age of 17, I was working long, hard hours, but I now had the opportunity to build a bond with my brother. We went to bars and night clubs in Biloxi, Gulfport, and Pascagoula. At the time, the drinking age was 18 and I had no

4

trouble buying booze. Working on the dredge had afforded me with a real-world education in the grown-up world.

I moved at the will of the company, which meant I moved from dredge to dredge wherever the jobs would take us all that year and into 1963. But my old pattern of dissatisfaction began to rear its ugly head and I began to grow tired of the long hours and hard work.

CHAPTER 2

As soon as I turned 18, I registered for the draft and started wondering where my life was really going. The prospect of going to Vietnam wasn't all that great, and I had begun to see that life on a dredge boat wasn't that wonderful either, so shortly after my birthday, I returned to high school in Aransas Pass and started my junior year once again.

Back in Aransas Pass, all of the students I had gone to school with since the 4th grade had already graduated. I may have learned a little more about the world, but I was two years behind in school. However, my final two years of high school were actually a lot of fun, and I have always been glad that I made the decision to return and graduate.

With my new attitude of self-assurance gained in the adult world of work, I made some solid friendships with my new classmates. There were six of us guys who hung around together. We called ourselves the "Boscos", a name derived from our daily activity of meeting at a guy's house to drink Bosco chocolate milk mix during our lunch hour from school. In those days, kids were allowed to leave the campus and eat wherever they wanted, which was usually French fries and gravy at the Bakery Café downtown, or a hamburger at Lands Drive-In, another popular hangout.

Times were so much simpler back then, and for the first time in my life, I was part of the "in" crowd. Our group included J.T. Marshall, the son of the local funeral home operator, Charlie Marshall. His home and his heart were always open to us, and some of my happiest memories came from my time spent there. Memories of Vi, a mother to all of us, of J.T.'s little brother, Bill, and his little sister, Marty Sue. All are gone now.

Then there was Joe Zorn. Joe lived with the Marshalls and was considered part of their family. He had a family of his own, but chose to live with the Marshalls. I never asked why. I figured if he wanted me to know, he'd tell me.

Marcel Calendar was also a member of our little clique. A darkly handsome guy from a well-to-do family, he was voted most handsome in school and had no trouble getting girls. Jerry McDonald was another one of the Boscos. He lived a ferry boat ride away over in Port Aransas, a small beach town on Mustang Island, and drove a beautiful green metal flaked '57 Chevy with black roll-and-pleat upholstery. The fifth member of our little group was William Grant, the son of a shrimper who worked on one of the many shrimp boats docked in Conn Brown Harbor.

And then there was a skinny little tag-along kid named John Lyman, the son of the new town doctor. He weighed about 100 pounds soaking wet and worked hard trying to be like us. The guys urged him to play football on the junior varsity team, and he survived it.

By this time my dad had moved our trailer to a lot he bought on the south side of Aransas Pass, so we were finally out of the trailer park. J.T., Joe, Marcel, Jerry, and William all played football on the varsity football team and had well-to-do parents. I was the only one out of the group who didn't play sports and came from the poorest family of them all.

Today, only John Lyman and I are still alive out of that group of boys. J.T. Marshal, William Grant, and Marcel Calendar all died too young, as did Jerry McDonald, who joined the Army and was killed in Vietnam. There's a baseball field named after him in Port Aransas, Texas.

My senior year of high school was probably one of the best years of my life. My father and brother were working closer to home and were around more often, and I was voted Most Popular Boy in school. The sad part about that was that everybody liked me, but me, and I was still envious of my friends. They had the looks, the money, the cars and clothes, the nice homes, well-to-do parents, pretty girlfriends and all the happiness they could stand while I stood on the sidelines, always on the outside looking in. But all that was about to change.

CHAPTER 3

In the summer of 1966, I turned 21. After trying my hand at college and working another series of jobs on tugs and shrimp boats, I bought my first motorcycle. A Honda 305 Scrambler. I had been riding other people's bikes for years, so at least I knew how to ride.

I had been fascinated with motorcycles all my life. I had a cousin in Louisiana who owned a Harley Hummer, a single cylinder bike manufactured during the late 1940's and fifties to compete with Triumph and BSA from England.

At the time, the Japanese still weren't major contributors in the bike world. I remember having a neighbor in the trailer park when I was about 15 who rode a big Harley Davidson Dresser. I was fascinated by the saddle bags, the huge tires, loud pipes and chromed parts. Basically, I was fascinated with the whole Harley mystique.

I would always watch him when he got ready to go somewhere, paying special attention to the starting procedure. Bikes in those days were all kick-started. The tricky part was the ignition and the timing. Old Harleys had the throttle on the right handlebar as all bikes do today. But on the left, there was another twist grip that would retard the timing, thus making it easier to start.

After the engine started up, you would twist the handgrip the other way to advance the timing, making the engine run normally. However, if you forgot to retard the timing, the kick-starter pedal would kick back against your leg, causing you to have a seriously fucked-up day.

One day, he saw me watching and told me that if I could start it, I could ride it. Without hesitating, I straddled the bike as I had seen him do so many times, turned the left handgrip to retard the timing, kicked it a few times to bring it up to the compression stroke, turned the key on, put my left knee on the seat and applied all my weight to my right leg and kicked it through. Instantly the engine came to life with that distinct, beautiful Harley sound. I twisted the left handgrip back and the engine smoothed out into a gentle idle. I smiled at him and said, "Now you got to show me how to shift the gears." He looked at me in astonishment and I learned that day that most Harley riders are truly men of their word, and my love for Harley Davidson motorcycles was born that day.

In the late summer of 1967, I tried to join the military but was turned down because I had only one kidney (the bad one had been removed by this time). With no real direction, I began hanging out with my old high school friend and fellow Boscos member, William Grant. He had been working on shrimp boats and had bought a 1966 Corvette. We drove around town and hung out at Lands Drive-In, smoking weed and just having fun. It was my first experience with drugs, and thus began a party that started in 1967 and didn't end until 1997.

I was 22 years old, had fifteen hours of college credit, and had a string of different jobs in which I was required to work a lot of long, hard hours for very little pay. I had been turned down by the military and had no ambition or idea of what I wanted to do with my life.

One afternoon, I was sitting on my motorcycle at a stop sign when I saw a guy with long hair ride past on a chopped Harley, and he was flying a set of Bandido colors on the back of a cut-off, Levi vest. The bright red and gold image of the Fat Mexican with his big sombrero on the back had a hypnotic effect on me.

I remember saying to myself that day, "I want to be like that guy". It was definitely a turning point. I have no idea why. Maybe it was because he seemed so free. Or maybe it was because he was part of something. Something exciting. Whatever it was, it was something I wanted in my life.

Although I continued to work on boats and lived at home, I now had a direction. I tried to customize my little Honda in a lame attempt at trying to make it look like a chopped Harley, with a purple paint job, high handlebars and upsweep exhausts. And then I met my first bikers.

I was at a local drive-in diner in Aransas Pass when some guys from a motorcycle club in Corpus Christi rode up. They called themselves Los Diablos, and after talking with them a while, they invited me to ride with them to Port Aransas. That night we went drinking and ended up partying on the beach, where I smoked some weed and became good friends with a member named Jerry Craig.

After they got to know me, I was initiated into their club and given a full set of colors. I began to spend more time in Corpus Christi, where I would stay at the Craig family house with Jerry, his mother and all five of his sisters and two brothers.

Jerry had a girlfriend, or "old lady" as women were referred to in biker society. The three of us lived in the garage with our bikes, tools, stereo system and black lights. We smoked lots of weed and ran around Corpus Christi, flying our colors and living what was fast becoming a new way of life and freedom.

In time, I found a guy who had an old Harley in parts, but it had a clear title and hopefully all the parts. Without a moment's hesitation, I traded my Honda for my first Harley, a 1951 Panhead basket case, and with the help of Jerry and some of the other members of the club, we managed to bring the old Harley back to life.

I called it my "Tractor". Instead of chrome, most of the shiny surfaces were just silver paint. I mounted an old Sportster gas tank on the top rail and cut down the stock rear fender. After that, I ran a suicide clutch, which is basically a pedal connected to a long rod called the clutch arm. When the pedal is pushed and held down with the left foot, the clutch will disengage. When it's released, the clutch springs engage the clutch and you best be ready to go. Hence the name "suicide clutch", because if you were sitting at a red light and your foot slipped off the pedal, you might find yourself headed for a real fucked-up day.

The shifting was done manually with your left hand using what was referred to as a "Jockey Shift" or "Butt Scratcher". The entire procedure took skill, nerve, balance, and lots of practice. Handling the bike while shifting is done with one hand on the throttle, and it's a delicate and dangerous dance of maneuvers that must all come together in the proper sequence. This is just one of the reasons riding in those days was referred to as "coffin cheating".

Soon, Jerry became president of the Los Diablos and I was elected vice-president. At the time, there were only seven full-time patch holders in our club, and in the summer of 1967, Jerry and I decided to move to Houston. We lived in a dumpy little motel on the north side of the city and found work hanging sheetrock in one of the new apartment complexes going up in the growing metropolis. On our days off, we rode around Houston flying our Los Diablos colors, me on my "Tractor" and Jerry on his Sportster, when he could get it started.

One day we were riding on Loop 610 on the north side of Houston when we encountered some Bandidos from the Houston chapter, including the founder of the club and the Bandidos' first El Presidente, Don Chambers, a man everyone referred to as Mother. As luck would have it, we had happened upon the entire Houston chapter, including all of the top-ranking members.

After talking with them for a while, we were invited to join them on a run to a farm outside of Yorktown, Texas, where they were due to meet up with some Bandidos from San Antonio and another club called "La Pack Rats", also from San Antonio.

For me, this was a dream come true. I was riding my bike in a huge pack of chopped Harleys, led by the premiere outlaw motorcycle club in the whole state of Texas. These were the formative years of the club, and I had been invited to be a part of a world I had been dreaming about since that day a few months earlier when I saw that guy ride past me flying his colors.

It didn't matter that I was fat, or that I lived in a trailer park, or that I had spent most of my life in fear of being judged or looked down upon by other people. I was being accepted. Unconditionally.

Later that night, with everyone gathered around the flames of a huge campfire reflecting off our bikes, we passed joints around, drank whiskey, and helped ourselves to free-flowing beer from kegs in ice tubs. The San Antonio chapter had brought their traditional five-gallon tins of tamales and bottles of picante sauce, which they passed around for everyone to enjoy. It was a scene straight out of one of the Hollywood B movies about outlaw California motorcycle gangs, so popular at the time. Movies like "The Wild Angels", starring Peter Fonda, Nancy Sinatra, and Bruce Dern. Only this was real, and I was a part of it. I felt alive for the first time in my life.

Later, a conference was called between Don Chambers and all the top-ranking Bandido officers, including those from Houston and San Antonio. During that conference, Don asked the other members to vote on bringing us and the other club from San Antonio into the Bandido nation. The vote was unanimous, and Jerry and I left the meeting with full Bandido colors.

We were instructed to return to Corpus as full patch Bandidos and inform our old club members that they had the opportunity to patch over, because as of now, no other colors could be flown in Corpus Christi. The Los Diablos were no longer a club. We were now Bandidos.

Upon our return, we broke the news to the other members and they all decided to patch over with us. Jerry became president of the chapter and I was voted in as vice-president. Before then, we were probably not taken very seriously. But all that changed pretty quickly when we began flying the Fat Mexican in Corpus and the surrounding cities in the Coastal Bend. We had respect, and no one dared to mess with us.

In those days, the motorcycle scene in Corpus was sparse, especially for Harleys. The only Harleys in town were the ones we rode. A couple of cops had them, as did a handful of citizens who rode them. It wasn't long before Jerry and I became skilled mechanics and well versed in building Harley choppers. With the help of some other brothers, we taught ourselves how to alter frame geometry to lower our machines. We learned how to extend front ends, as was the style at the time.

The industry was in its infancy then, and there weren't a lot of aftermarket parts available for customizers. Out of necessity, we quickly learned how to build one-of-a-kind parts for our bikes. We became so skilled, other riders and patch holders were soon seeking us out to work on their bikes and teach them as well.

In the early days of the club, the motorcycle was the focal point. Naturally, we would party at the drop of a hat, and I'd be lying if I said there weren't a few criminal elements, but the lure and attraction to the Bandido lifestyle was never rooted in criminal activity. For one thing, we were too visible, and our colors were magnets for cops. The basic attraction for the lifestyle we were living in those early formative years was the motorcycle lifestyle. Everything was centered around riding our Harleys, and most of our money came from our jobs as part-time mechanics or in construction as laborers.

Some of us had old ladies that danced in topless bars. They usually made good money on tips, and every now and then I'd sell a little weed. However, we smoked most of what we got our hands on before we ever made any profit.

At no other time in my life have I ever been able to experience the freedom that was available to me and my brothers back then. I had been locked into a world of stifling responsibility since the age of 10, without the skills and coping mechanisms to deal with it. I had found a new way of life. I had found a way to be successfully irresponsible. I was no longer Norman, the fat kid from the trailer park with so many fears and doubts about myself and the world. I had been given a new name. I was Aransas, the Bandido. I had respect from all my peers in the club. I had brothers that I had never met from cities and states I had never been to. And it was that way for all the years of my active membership.

I was accepted. My opinions were valued. I held every ranking position in every chapter in which I became a member. We were always ready and willing to help each other in any way. The feelings of traveling in a large group of motorcycles over hundreds of miles and meeting with other members after a long hard ride was better than any drug. The pains and aches of riding rigid frame motorcycles melted away in the hugs and greetings of brothers we hadn't seen in months or years.

When our machines broke down, there were no bike shops or Harley dealerships in almost every town like there are today. We had to fix our problems ourselves; most of the time right on the side of the road. Our skills and knowledge of our bikes was all that some of us really had to offer. I learned to diagnose problems, and I knew the solutions to get an ailing bike back on the road again.

There was pride in knowing that my bike always started right away. I kept it maintained and was always willing to share this with my brothers so they would also know the pride and honor of being able to maintain their own machines. This knowledge, among other things, was a binding force for us in those days.

In the Spring of 1968, I decided to move back to Houston and became active in the Houston chapter. I lived in Don Chambers' house on Eastwood Drive along with a few other brothers. His house was always open to anyone in the club that needed a place to stay.

For a time, I worked as a longshoreman on the docks in Houston. We spent long hours unloading train cars and filling pallets to go into the cargo holds of ships. Sometimes it was the other way around and we unloaded cargo into railroad cars. Basically, things were going well. Really good. We had our bikes, we had weed, we had women, and we had each other. A few months after I moved back to Houston, we moved into the mansion.

CHAPTER 4

On the south side Houston, there was a large undeveloped property on Wayside Drive. Behind a pair of ornate steel gates, an aged paved road twisted through a forest of palm trees to an imposing mansion.

The mansion itself was an architectural treasure, and behind it was a structure known as a carriage house before the days of automobiles. In its later days, it became the garage area for the vehicles owned by the family that had once lived in this unbelievable urban oasis in the middle of metropolis Houston.

Off to one side of the carriage house was a two-story structure with what looked like stalls where horses had been kept. Above the stalls were individual small apartments referred to as slave quarters.

As it turned out, the present caretaker was a Bandido in the Houston chapter named Bill S., who had given all of his brothers with no place to go permission to live in the slave quarters. Bill also let us use the carriage house as a garage area to work on our motorcycles. There were always around ten or fifteen Bandidos living there at one time or another, but we never ventured into the main house or any of the other houses on the property.

We paid Bill as much as we could for rent and helped each other when it came to food and supplies. Many of us earned our keep by helping to maintain the grounds or working on bikes for anyone willing to pay us.

However, most of the time our sustenance was a result of our contributions to help each other. When one brother had money, he naturally shared it with the others. Much like the winos who chipped in to buy booze in the days of my Uncle Pot.

The main gate into the property appeared to be locked, but on closer inspection, those in the know could open it quite easily, and with all the Bandidos on the property, security wasn't an issue.

One afternoon, several of us rode up to the gated entrance on our motorcycles and discovered that the gates were actually locked. While one brother slithered under the gate to see what was up, the rest of us waited outside with our bikes lined up against the curb facing out. We had learned over time to park like this to provide a quick getaway in case of trouble.

As we sat there, a Houston police cruiser drove by, obviously suspicious about our presence in front of a long-abandoned mansion. When our brother returned and opened the gate, we entered in ignorant bliss, unaware that the wheels of law enforcement were beginning to spin against us.

As it turned out, the police had decided that they had discovered the long sought-after hideout of the notorious Bandido motorcycle gang, so later that afternoon armed with search warrants, they swooped in to look for stolen motorcycles, firearms and illegal drugs.

Unaware of what was about to happen, I was in a deep sleep in one of the air-conditioned rooms in the slave quarters, where I had been staying for several weeks. I awoke to a Houston police officer with a gun pointed right at me and telling me I was under arrest for a variety of charges, including trespassing and possession of stolen property.

There were about a dozen brothers on the property that day and we were all hauled out in handcuffs to sit on the curb, while the newspapers and television reporters had a banner day reporting the breakup of a vast motorcycle theft ring involving the Bandidos motorcycle gang.

This was my first arrest and first time on the six o'clock news. I say first because it wouldn't be my last. After the reporters were done with their pictures, we were taken to the main Houston police station on Reiser Street, where we were booked and crowded into a large holding tank with everyone else who had been arrested in Houston in the last thirty-six hours.

Holding tanks are large, uncomfortable, crowded, and can be quite dangerous. Needless to say, with a dozen Bandidos in one holding tank, we were the controlling power. The others gave us a very wide berth with the sudden realization that they were now the ones in danger, not us.

I was approached by a skinny little Mexican pachuco who had snuck a marijuana joint into jail. He was too afraid to smoke it in the holding tank, so he gave it to us and we allowed him to sit at our table while we all got high together in the Houston city jail.

We were eventually bailed out by Bill S., and when the case finally came to trial, the prosecution made the mistake of calling the estate representative as a witness, who just happened to be Bill. When the prosecutor asked him about the fact that we were all on this property, he testified that he was well aware of our presence and he had given us permission to be there. We were, he went on to explain, workers hired by his employer to help maintain security of the vast estate.

The motorcycle parts were all registered and none of the engine numbers or part numbers were on any lists of stolen property. No weapons other than our legal knives were ever found, and the only drug found was beer in the refrigerators and whiskey in the cabinets. Needless to say, the charges were summarily dropped and we walked out of the courtroom with huge grins on our faces.

CHAPTER 5

During my life as a Houston Bandido, I met brothers who I became close to in my new life. I remember a guy named Crazy. When I met him, he had just become a patch holder and was still going to college. I remember he would strap his books to the back of his Sportster and go to classes. He eventually dropped out and his whole life became involved with the club. He was a master at sharpening knives and carried a Buck knife as sharp as a shaving razor.

One night, we were pulled over on the south side of Houston on Telephone Road by about four Houston police officers. One of the officers took Crazy's knife, opened it up and ran his thumb down the edge of the blade, nearly cutting the end of his thumb off. As he held a handkerchief to his bleeding thumb, he looked at Crazy and said, "God damnit, boy! What do you do with this knife?" Crazy smiled back at him and said, "I mostly just sharpen it."

Since none of us had any outstanding warrants and we hadn't done anything wrong, they had to let us go. As we rode off, we couldn't keep from smiling at the cop holding his bleeding thumb.

Then there was Apple, a little freckle-faced white guy with shocking red hair worn in a huge Afro. Apple was from New Jersey and always rode old Flathead Harleys. In the mid-60s, these bikes had been out of production for over thirty years, and he was constantly looking for parts. Nevertheless, he refused to ride anything else. He died on a BMW in 1973. I've always thought he should have stuck with the Flatheads.

I met one of my dearest friends and brothers during this time. He was a giant of a man we all called Tank. With a pair of piercing blue eyes and weighing in at over three hundred pounds, he had long black hair with a full black beard and stood six-foot-six. He also had a heart as big as Texas.

We eventually became members of the Nomad chapter of the Bandidos and traveled as far as Washington State and South Dakota, plus all the states in between with the exception of California, which was Hells Angels territory. They stayed out of our territory, and we stayed out of theirs.

Because of our size, we were often asked if we were wrestlers, so we always said yes and received great welcomes ... welcomes we wouldn't have received if the people asking had known we were really Bandidos.

Tank had this uncanny ability to be a master wheeler-dealer. I can never recall a time when he didn't own at least one very nice Harley and at least one very nice truck or car. I remember one of his favorite sayings was, "I've been on top a thousand times." Whenever he managed to fall from the top, it never took him long to get back up there again. I believe one of his secrets was that he never really got attached to his possessions.

I remember Fuzzy from the Houston chapter, and Jimbo. There was Alley Cat, Apache, Jesus, Ronnie Hodge, Sarge, Spanky, Whitey, Deadweight, Geronimo, and many others. They were my new family, and I loved my brothers no matter who they were or where they were from.

Members of the Galveston chapter usually rode and partied with the Houston brothers and vice versa. There was also a chapter in the Port Arthur area called the Jefferson County chapter, as well as one in Beaumont that had a brother who was a deaf-mute that we all called Dummy.

This was a time of riding, partying, meeting new members and becoming immersed into the Bandido culture, and we could always be found in an area of Houston known as Allen's Landing, an old warehouse district near Buffalo Bayou. Many of the old warehouse buildings had been redeveloped into head shops, bars and other retail outlets that appealed to the burgeoning hippie lifestyle of those days.

It was a time when the Haight-Ashbury area was thriving in San Francisco and the hippie culture was popping up all over the country, and Allen's Landing was the center of the hippie scene in Houston.

The 10-block area of Allen's Landing was populated with psychedelic night clubs. The bars were packed every night of the week, and we were the top dogs in this scene. We never had to pay cover charges and seldom had to pay for our drinks. The heady aroma of marijuana drifted through the air and drugs were everywhere. So was free love and a whole lot of other promiscuous behavior. This was decades before HIV, and the worst we had to worry about was a bad case of "The Clap".

The music and melodies of The Doors, Jimi Hendrix, Janis Joplin, Steppenwolf, Led Zeppelin and all the other iconic groups and bands of the era mixed nightly with the straight pipe rumbles from Harley exhausts. The cops just drove by and gave us dirty looks but usually left us alone as long as we weren't causing any trouble.

Food and drink also wasn't much of an issue in those days. All the little cafes and eating establishments were happy to feed us and let us have our way in their businesses. We had a way of policing ourselves and making sure we didn't screw up a good thing once we found a place that liked us or were too afraid to say anything about us being in their establishments. Even though some of them were obviously a little uncomfortable with us around, we usually enjoyed a symbiotic relationship with them by providing security in exchange for food and drinks.

In a hedonistic atmosphere like Allen's Landing, we were always meeting and picking up women. An old saying goes like this: "Ladies love outlaws". And we definitely put this axiom to the test on a nightly basis.

It was during this time that I met my first "old lady". I met Judy somewhere in the madness of Allen's Landing, and although I was developing into the man I had always wanted to be, I was still pretty uneducated when it came to relationships with women.

We were all sitting around in a circle, sharing a joint, when our eyes met. She was 21 years old and from a well-to-do Houston family. One of those rebellious types that had always had everything provided for them and had always wondered what living a different lifestyle would be like. In Allen's Landing, she had found out. She had become a speed freak, adept at conning people out of their money.

We hit it off right away and she rode back with me to a garage apartment on Kirby Drive, where I was staying with another brother named Geronimo. Most of our time was spent living the lifestyle to the fullest. On Sundays, we would all go to a park on the southeast side of Houston to watch free concerts and get high with the hippies. I sometimes sold bags of weed called "lids" to them, and then we would help them smoke the stuff they just bought from us.

It was the summer of 1968. The summer of Vietnam, the Democratic National Convention, hippies, peace marches, love-ins, riots and Ohio, the great tune by Crosby, Stills, Nash and Young. It was a time to be young and wild in America and to be involved at the pinnacle of the outlaw motorcycle pyramid in Texas.

Our red and gold nation was expanding at an alarming and exhilarating rate, with more chapters in more cities and states every month. Whether we rode in packs of 30, or there were only two or three of us, everyone noticed. We were objects of admiration and envy, as well as ones of distrust and fear.

19

I believe the fact that we did pretty much whatever we wanted to do was probably the greatest source of fear from those who watched us from a distance. We were judged by the standards of the recent Hollywood B movies that painted us as lunatics that came into small towns and raped and pillaged and rode off with loads of booty and all the town's women strapped to our bikes. And there were times we even fostered that image to our advantage.

In actuality, if anyone ever rode away with us, they did so of their own choosing just to escape the mundane existence of their lives. In October of that year, I felt I needed a break from all the partying and decided to go back to work on one of the dredges with my father. Judy and I loaded all our stuff up in a U-Haul and moved to an apartment in Pascagoula, Mississippi with my parents.

To say my parents were from the old school was an understatement, and they weren't too thrilled with Judy and I sleeping in the same bed together under their roof. To assuage their feelings, and maybe even provide some indication that I was turning over a new leaf, I asked Judy to marry me.

In truth, I didn't truly love her because I had no concept of what real love was really about. Inside, I was still the insecure, scared fat kid, especially around my parents. Because marriage was still the norm of the day, I felt we should probably get hitched, so we rode to a little town called Eight Mile Alabama and found a justice of the peace to marry us.

We moved into a little rent trailer on the outskirts of Pascagoula and I continued to work on the dredge, but I was still a Bandido. Our life was surreal. My bike was in boxes and we were hauling it around with us while I was trying to be a husband in the same straight society I had tried to get away from. All the while the memories of the freedom and wildness of the Houston Bandido scene were still fresh in my mind, and they were calling out to me.

When the dredge boat job I was on ended, we moved to Little Rock, Arkansas, where I went to work with my father on another dredge. My father was a troubleshooter and was sent to jobs where the captain was not keeping up with the contract and the company was losing money. He was always able to bring them out of the red and get them back to making a profit.

His lengthy experience enabled him to handle any problem, and for a man with an eighth-grade education, he was a highly respected dredge boat captain. I was proud of him. We were working on the Arkansas River about 30 miles from Little Rock. I was running a swamp buggy that

20

we used to move pipe for the discharge line on the banks of the river. The hours went fast and the work was steady, and most importantly, I was able to get high all the time.

When the drive back and forth to the boat got too expensive, we moved closer to the river in a little town called Mayflower, Arkansas. The people we rented the little house from were so redneck that they evicted us for putting up a Rolling Stones poster in the living room. Little did they know how much weed we were smoking in their crappy little rent house.

By now, I had had enough of this strait-laced life away from my Bandido brothers, so we packed up our stuff and moved back to a small apartment on the south side of Houston. Thanks in large part to our arrival, the apartment house complex quickly became a Bandido hangout, and soon nearly every apartment was occupied by a Bandido, and those who weren't Bandidos only got to stay because we allowed them to live amongst us. Usually they were drug dealers, and we offered them a level of protection that they gladly accepted.

I was never very popular with Judy's mother or her other family members. Her mother hauled out the old, tired rhetoric about me not being worthy of her daughter and obviously being beneath them on the social ladder, and she devoted most of her time to trying to split us up. She once sent me a copy of her will and testament and pointed out the fact that in the event of her death, I would receive no more and no less than one dollar.

I was happy to be with my brothers again, and I enjoyed the life even more than before. We built bikes in the apartment's garages on a 24-hour basis, and weed and other drugs were plentiful. We were always partying in one apartment or another and Houston was our apple, a fact we relished to the fullest extent.

Aside from life at the apartment house complex, many of our days were devoted to riding and partying in different areas of the city. During this time, there were some small biker clubs that tried to start up, but as soon as we found out, we pulled their colors and made them break up.

You see, when you allow another club to ride in your territory, and they do something illegal, all any witness ever sees is a guy on a Harley wearing a vest with some kind of emblem on the back. When another club is allowed on your turf, you have to fade their heat and possibly take the fall for any crime they might have committed. When there is only one club in an area, then the colors become familiar to everyone and nobody winds up having to go to jail for something another club did.

CHAPTER 6

In the early months of 1970, I decided to move to the San Antonio chapter and got permission from the Houston chapter to transfer. I had always liked San Antonio. The Hill Country north of the city is a beautiful area filled with clear rivers and state parks, and to me, that part of Texas always reminded me of another state.

It's much more crowded now, but back then we had the Hill Country roads mostly to ourselves. Interstate 35 is the highway that runs from San Antonio up through Austin and on to Dallas. Between San Antonio and Austin, the Hill Country rises up in the west. To the east, the land is mostly flat farmland all the way to the piney woods of East Texas.

Needless to say, I relished the new environment and the brotherhood in the San Antonio chapter. Judy and I lived with a brother named Chuco, who had a garage apartment on the south-central side of San Antonio, the center of the universe for the hippies and drug culture back then.

The bars had psychedelic light shows, black lights, strobe lights and live music blasting away every night. The party never ended and we were definitely in the middle of it all. Two of the brothers had opened a head shop on Main Street near the college, so we always had a place to hang out and basically ruled the entire neighborhood.

Life then was intoxicating and exhilarating. Judy could panhandle all the money we needed on a daily basis. The weed and acid were free most of the time and I could always pick up some cash by selling a little weed to the hippies and college students.

San Antonio at that time seemed like a sleepy little Mexican village with a weed smoker on every block. I was enthralled and mesmerized by the city and the people who lived there. Houston was always like a combat zone. You always had the feeling of being on patrol and had to keep a constant lookout as if you were a recon platoon in the freaking Mekong Delta. We never knew where the enemy was or when he would strike.

In the San Antonio of the early 1970s, we were accepted as just another part of the color and atmosphere in the city. I suppose it was the name Bandidos that endeared us to the Hispanic community. Then again, it could have been the wild Texas outlaw streak that had been such a big part of this region back in the 19th century.

I remember my brothers Batman, Panhead, Boo Boo, Bones, Big Bill, Rocky, Scosh, Royce, Big Bobby, Big Daddy, Chuco, Chan and Kendall. There were others whose names I've unfortunately forgotten. I was the closest with Batman, Big Bobby, Kendall and Chuco. After we left Chuco's place, Judy and I lived in an old Ford Econoline van in Big Daddy's back yard. I had traded my pickup truck to Tank for the van and we put bunks in the back and slept there at night while using Big Daddy's facilities in the house.

We usually cooked outside on barbecue pits and everybody pitched in to make enough food for everyone. We worked on our own bikes in Big Daddy's garage as well as doing work for other people. It was funny to us that the cops and everyone else assumed we were these big-time drug dealers with tons of money, when in fact we were living mostly hand to mouth and day to day, riding our bikes and just having fun.

Of course, there were other drugs around besides weed. Drugs like speed, which was never really my thing. I always preferred drugs that relaxed me and didn't keep me awake for days on end. Cocaine was around too, but I hardly ever used it in those days. Smoking crack was unheard of at the time.

In the spring of 1970, the president of the Bandidos, Don Chambers, became concerned with the increase of people shooting drugs in the hippie community and instituted a national by-law prohibiting intravenous drug use by any patch holder. Any member caught using a needle would be kicked out of the club in bad standing, lose his colors, motorcycle and any possessions the club wanted to take from him, plus he would be severely dealt with by the other patch holders.

Labor Day has always been a mandatory event for all Bandido members and must be attended wherever it is held. In 1970, it was held in San Antonio at a private rental location called the Domino Ranch, about two miles south of Loop 410 in San Antonio.

The event is usually held from Saturday until Tuesday, and the party is non-stop. I remember meeting brothers from Louisiana, Arkansas, Washington State, plus many from new chapters that had sprung up in Texas. This was a growing period for the club, and we were definitely growing.

24

As host city for the run, we went all out in putting on a good party for the brothers. Everyone was handed a bag of weed on arrival and the beer trucks were delivering beer kegs on a daily basis. The San Antonio chapter also provided their signature food dish; 5-gallon cans of tamales and gallons of Pace picante sauce.

We camped out there for the entire weekend, enjoying the camaraderie and getting to know one another. On Monday afternoon I went into a blackout and awakened with Judy in the middle of a field on Tuesday. We were the only people left at the site. I don't remember what happened during that time, but I guess everything went alright since I wasn't in any trouble when I got back to town and contacted my brothers.

CHAPTER 7

After Labor Day, Judy and I decided to go to Corpus Christi and stay with Jerry Craig and Frenchy while I built a new bike. Actually, it was the same bike but I just wanted to make it different. It was the style at that time to drastically alter the geometry of our bikes and still have ridable machines, so after I took my bike apart, I had Jerry's welder neighbor cut and rake the neck on the frame so I could extend the front end another ten inches, making my bike about seven feet long from axle to axle.

I painted the frame black and had what they called a mustang tank that I painted black with flames in shades of red, orange, and yellow. I also did some engine work to keep it running and added a new rear fender and tall sissy bar for a backrest for Judy. Bikes at that time were totally for function and had no extra parts. I had no blinkers, floorboards, bags or any non-essential items, which is why they were usually called "choppers". With only a taillight, headlight and one mirror, and with no front brake or front fender, it actually turned out really nice for a no-frills chopper.

When it was completed, I decided to make a run to San Antonio to show my new bike off to my brothers. The trip went well until I reached the outskirts of San Antonio on Loop 410. I was 5 miles from Big Bill's house going about 65 miles per hour when it felt like a huge hand slapped me in the back and knocked me off my bike.

I hit the asphalt and rolled and tumbled for quite a way before landing on my knees in time to watch my bike slide off the road and hit a light pole. This was the first of three high-speed crashes I would be involved in on a motorcycle.

At first, I thought that someone had shot me off my bike. But after I determined there weren't any bullet holes in me, I discovered that the two nuts that held my rear fender to the frame had vibrated loose. When they fell off, the fender met the tire and the sissy bar came forward and hit me in the back, knocking me off the bike and saving me from hitting the light pole.

My bike had damage to the headlight, tank, handlebars, and of course the rear fender and sissy bar. I was sore and had some road rash, but luckily, I wasn't injured badly. Within a few days, I had my bike up and running again.

For the remainder of that year, we lived with various brothers around San Antonio before eventually renting a little one-bedroom house on the south side of San Antonio in a predominantly Mexican neighborhood off Roosevelt Avenue. There we met a girl who owned a 1969 Volkswagen Beetle that she was unable to make payments on, so me, Tank, Grubby and our old ladies decided to take a trip up to Washington State and see how the new chapter was doing up there.

I made a deal with the girl who owned the Volkswagen. She agreed to give me a week to get to Washington before reporting the car as being stolen. Tank, Grubby, their old ladies and Grubby's dog all rode in Tanks truck with the bikes, while Judy and I followed in the Volkswagen on a non-stop trip fueled with black mollies to keep us awake.

I remember passing through some mountains in Oregon and seeing a big dog running alongside the car. He was only one of the creatures I saw popping up in the road ahead of me due to the effects of the amphetamines. Luckily, we made it safely to Washington and I sold the car for 300 dollars with no title.

We spent that spring of '70 living in Bremerton, Port Orchard, Kent, and Everett Washington. The bike I had brought along didn't have a title, so I traded it for an older Harley with a clear title and built another bike from that one.

We were never rolling in money, but our needs were met just the same. In the early summer of 1970, Judy got a phone call from her mother and was told her grandmother was in the hospital and not expected to live. I put Judy on an airplane for Houston the next morning and I never saw or heard from her again.

None of my calls were ever answered, and when I got back to Texas later that summer, I finally got her mother to talk to me. She informed me that Judy had divorced me and that she never wanted to see or hear from me again. I really didn't know you could be divorced and not even be present or sign any kind of papers. After the call, I rode to the dam on Lake Travis and threw my wedding ring into the lake. To this day, I have never heard anything from Judy.

That summer, I lived outside of Austin with another brother who had a shop in Austin and spent most of my time partying with the Austin Bandido chapter. That summer, I was also accepted as a member in the Nomad chapter of the Bandidos. This is a chapter that has no set home base. Basically, members travel from chapter to chapter, taking care of problems and assisting in the formation of new chapters.

At the time, requirements to become a Nomad were five years of membership and unanimous approval from the other chapter members. I no longer flew the Corpus Christi rocker on my colors. I now flew the Nomad rocker. Back in the early years of the club, patched members flew rockers designating the cities they were from. Later on, city rockers were exchanged for state rockers because the club was the only recognized one-percenter club and claimed ownership of the entire state. Any other club that used one of our state rockers was in violation of the biker code and faced stiff penalties.

Tank, Grubby and I were now Nomads, and we became well known within the club as we traveled around the country. During my stay in Austin, I traded the bike I built in Washington for a bike another brother built. This bike was a hot rod but could be temperamental at times, so I traded it to another brother for a more reliable bike.

I remember the first trip I made on the new bike was back down to Corpus to visit my old brothers. I pulled into a shop that St. John ran on the south side of Corpus and will never forget when I turned the bike off. The radio was playing Rod Stewart's "Maggie Mae". I got off my bike, took my headlight out of the housing, pulled out an ounce of marijuana and we began partying. That memory is as vivid as if it happened yesterday.

During that stay in Corpus Christi, some of us brothers went over to Port Aransas. I had a friend from my earlier days before joining the club who owned a bar, and we were all partying there. Sometimes guys who had drunk too much artificial courage would try to mess with us, and since the owner had known me for years, I was the go-to guy to curtail any problems we might have with the regular customers. I had already managed to stop some brothers from beating a few people up while we were there, and while I was defusing another situation, the police were called.

The bar was kind of like an old western bar, with a long wooden porch out front. When the responding officer drove up, he stepped out of his patrol car all alone with a sawed-off shotgun. I saw right away that it was my old friend from high school, John Lyman, the skinny tag-along kid who weighed a hundred pounds soaking wet, and he was now a full-grown man and a cop.

He has related to me since that night that he was very relieved to see me there when he pulled up by himself in his patrol car and heard what he believed were the thuds of guns and knives hitting the wood planks on the porch and saw all those Bandidos staring back at him. Satisfied that I had everything under control, he left and we cleared out.

On the way back to Corpus Christi, we had to travel down an 18-mile stretch of road known as the Island Road. This is a straight-line road with the Gulf of Mexico on the east side and Corpus Christi Bay on the west side of the road. I had managed to get a little drunk before leaving with a brother named Red, and we were traveling about 90 mph when we passed another brother who was on the shoulder with a flat tire.

He had built a little fire for light and as we roared past him, I thought his bike was on fire. I was in the outside lane and Red was to my left on the inside lane. As we flew past, I looked to my right and my bike drifted left into Red's lane. My front tire touched his rear tire and instantly my bike went down on its right side and I slid down the road, finally coming to a stop along the sandy shoulder in the high grass and sticker burrs.

This was my second high-speed crash, and I managed to walk away with nothing more than a few bruises and road rash on my knees and arms. My bike had cosmetic damage, and after I had healed enough to work on it, I had it up and running again within a couple days.

On August 3, 1970, hurricane Celia hit the Texas Gulf Coast. This was a major and extremely devastating hurricane. I watched from my brother Jerry's house as the wind was blowing the rain parallel to the street. During the eye of the storm, Tank, Jerry and I rode around town in a truck and witnessed the aftermath of the first part of this major storm. We saw boats on land that had been thrown out of the bay next to stores, houses, trailers and big 18-wheeler trucks, all completely demolished.

On the way back to Jerry's house, the wind turned from the other direction after the eye had passed and we could feel the back of the truck being lifted off the ground. We finally made it back to Jerry's and somehow managed to sleep through the remainder of the storm.

Jerry's house received no major damage, while others on the same block were totally demolished. For days after the storm, there was no infrastructure. We lived in the back yard in tents with the relentless mosquitoes, while the military delivered ice and fresh water. We had no running water to bathe with and we all received vouchers from the government to buy tents, clothing, stoves, lamps, sleeping bags, ice chests and other living supplies.

Our motorcycles were the only means of transportation in the Coastal Bend area due to road destruction and blockages from downed trees and power lines, so we all volunteered with the Red Cross. We were issued travel permits allowing us to deliver supplies and medicine on our bikes to surrounding towns that had come under National Guard quarantine to prevent looting and stealing. After a return to normalcy, the Red Cross threw a big party with an awards ceremony for all the Bandidos, and we received volunteer pins which we proudly wore on our colors.

CHAPTER 8

A few months after the hurricane, Tank, Grubby and I decided to take a trip to El Paso, where a new chapter was just being formed. We loaded our bikes and Grubby's dog, Rocky, into Tank's truck and off we went. While there, I met a girl named Lynn who was dancing at a bar outside of town and I hooked up with her. After she became my old lady, I had another source of income from her dancing.

People who aren't part of our world don't understand this. It's really no different from a husband and wife both working to support themselves. It was the same for us. She worked at her job, and I worked at mine. It was a mutual thing, and no one was being taken advantage of.

While in El Paso, one of their members was kicked out of the club. Naturally, we kept everything he had, including his motorcycle. Later, this guy called the police and told them that the El Paso Bandidos had stolen his bike. Once again, I was in the wrong place at the wrong time.

The police raided the house where we were staying and arrested everyone there for possession of stolen property. I slept most of the time I was in jail and we were bailed out two days later. All of the charges were eventually dropped after a couple of local Bandido brothers had a meeting with the guy and reminded him that when he joined the club, he had voluntarily agreed that his bike would be forfeited if he ever left the club in bad standing. He had a sudden moment of clarity and dropped the charges.

I really enjoyed El Paso, with Mount Franklin in the middle separating the city into East and West. We would say we were going flying and ride up the mountain. Upon reaching the top, the road began the descent on a long series of graceful banked switchbacks into the other side of town. As we started down from the highest point, I would put my bike in neutral, reach down and cut the key off the ignition and coast the rest of the way down the mountain. What a feeling. No engine sounds, no pipes, just wheels on pavement with the cool West Texas breeze in my face. It was as close to flying as a man could get and still be on the ground.

Shortly after that, we decided to return to San Antonio. We loaded back into Tank's truck, except this time I brought Lynn with me. We moved to a house on the northeast side of San Antonio with Big Bobby, and I put Lynn to work right away to insure some type of income.

Additionally, I had a deal with another brother to provide protection for some girls who were working as prostitutes. I also had money coming in from motorcycle parts and selling a little weed every now and then.

It escapes me now, but Lynn decided to leave me for some odd reason, so I remained in the house with Big Bobby and some other brothers. Around this time, I began experiencing a lot of pain in my lower back. When it got too bad, I began taking more and more pain killers.

Eventually, I had to go to a doctor and was diagnosed with ruptured discs in my lower back. The doctor attributed this condition to years of being overweight, plus years of riding rigid frame motorcycles.

I underwent a surgical procedure called a laminectomy, where the ruptured discs are repaired and the fragments are removed to eliminate the possibility of causing pain to the spinal cord. The operation was successful, but the patient was uncooperative. I didn't lose any weight and continued to ride a rigid frame Harley. I also continued to take pain killers for many more years.

In the early part of 1972, I was living on the couch at a house in the Garden District of San Antonio, where my Bandido brother, Deadweight, was living. I remember that winter because it snowed that year, a rare occurrence in San Antonio. It was there that I first met some Pagans from the East Coast. They were here under permission of some National Bandido officers. These guys had some stuff called "killer weed", which was basically parsley or real weed mixed with PCP. Nevertheless, this was a powerful and dangerous combination to smoke. I remember one time when I was lying on the couch in Batman's house, smoking that weed under the bright living room light while the TV and stereo were both playing, and the loudest thing in the house was the light!

Every time I smoked KW, it was as if I picked up right where I had left off the last time I smoked the stuff. In one instance, I thought I saw demons and was being chased down San Pedro Avenue in San Antonio by the devil. We were all in a VW bus and I leaned out the window and fired a 30-caliber machine gun toward an imaginary Satan I believed was hot on our tail.

I didn't hit anybody, thank God, but I can still find the pock marks from the bullets in the underpass at the intersection of Hildebrand and San Pedro. I never smoked KW again after that episode.

When I drank and rode my motorcycle, I rode very fast and dangerously. The combination of alcohol is dangerous for me because when I'm drinking, my motorcycle runs so much better. I'm unable to hear any sounds the engine may be making and it always seems to be running as smooth as glass. On the other hand, when I'm smoking weed, I ride very slowly and cautiously. It is as if I can hear every sound my engine is making and can feel every vibration.

It was during this time that every hippie in San Antonio, as well as a lot of the college kids, were taking LSD, and we were no different. Sometimes, I would take LSD and ride. When I did that, I was never able to stop at red lights or stop signs because I always had the feeling that something was following me, and if I stopped, it would get me. I am extremely lucky I was never hit by someone while running a light or stop sign. I still took a lot of LSD but never had a fun trip. I suppose the trip is contingent on the situation you are in when the drug is ingested. I lived in a dangerous and violent world, and I believe my trips reflected this on a grand scale.

Around this time, I had my bike repainted by a local painter in San Antonio. He painted it a pearl yellow and molded a skull face into the top of the gas tank. In the late winter of 1973, I was riding with another brother to a place out on the Guadalupe River, about 40 miles north of San Antonio. By now, Lynn had returned and was riding on the back of my bike with our dog in her bag.

I was running a stock springer front end with a mechanical front brake and we had just crossed the Guadalupe River bridge on 281 when the brake boss bolt vibrated loose and fell out. This caused the drum to spin around and subsequently tightened the front brake cable, causing the brake shoe to expand and lock the front brake.

I did a nosedive at about 80 mph, while Lynn and the dog flew over my head. She landed on her face and knocked her three front upper teeth out. The dog was scared but unharmed. I wound up under the bike for a few hundred feet and had some major scrapes and road rash, but nothing was broken.

We were taken to Bexar County Hospital and treated and released. Lynn had to get her teeth replaced at the free clinic, and I just laid around until I felt good enough to rebuild my bike again. Needless to say, the fancy new paint job had been trashed and I had to replace the front end.

33

This was my third high-speed crash. In the years since, I have gone down a few more times, but they were mostly low-speed crashes. I still ride a Harley today, but a few years ago I decided to start wearing a full-face helmet. I figure that after fifty-five years of riding Harleys, the odds are eventually going to catch up to me. It's a fatalistic view, but at age seventy-seven, I don't see any real reason I should give up doing something that brings me so much pleasure.

CHAPTER 9

Shortly after the accident, Lynn left again and Tank, Grubby and I decided to move up to Oklahoma City. There were no Bandidos there at the time and we wanted to show the colors and see what kind of reaction we would get from local clubs like the Rogues or the Outlaws.

We got a little house on the southwest side of town and I met a girl named Cindy from Dallas. Cindy was into some pretty heavy drug use and shot a lot of heroin and opiates. I was with her for a while, but she was not a good money maker and I had to get away from the needles. Besides, we had a by-law, and I wasn't too keen on the idea of losing everything over her and a shot of dope.

As soon as she was out of the scene, Lynn came to Oklahoma City to join me. I immediately put her to work dancing in a topless bar with Tank and Grubby's old ladies. Life was pretty good there for a while. We would take the old ladies to work and then go riding or hang around the house, getting stoned or working on our bikes.

Before we left San Antonio, I had traded the last bike I built for an old San Antonio police dresser. It was black and white, and amazingly, it still had the siren and red lights attached. After I rode it to Oklahoma, I removed all the police stuff and rebuilt the engine.

Tank had a 1945 Harley Knucklehead chopper that was bright yellow with a raked frame and long Sportster front end. The term Knucklehead was used to identify the first overhead valve engines Harley Davidson produced from 1936 to 1949. The rocker assemblies were in a large aluminum casting on the heads and resembled a fist, hence the term, Knucklehead.

The engine was built the same year I was born and was still in good running condition. Tank wanted my bike because it was newer and more comfortable, so we traded and I became the proud owner of the Big Banana, a bike that turned out to be my favorite. I have the engine numbers tattooed on my back; 45FL1107.

Life was pretty good in Oklahoma City, but we quickly grew bored and decided to move to South Dakota, where some new chapters were starting up and it was our job as Nomads to check them out. We used a fictitious drivers license to rent a big U-Haul and loaded it up with everything we owned. The old ladies and Grubby's dog rode in Tank's Oldsmobile, and off we went to Rapid City, South Dakota.

Upon arrival in Rapid City, we unloaded the truck at a house we had rented and left it on the side of the Interstate. Lynn and I lived in the basement with all my Bandido collectibles and a Nazi flag on the wall. The bed was a mattress on the floor covered in silk sheets and pillows. This was sectioned off with a large Persian rug hanging from the floor joists above, prompting me to call our part of the house the "Temple of the Insultin' Sultan".

Lynn was working in a local titty bar along with the other old ladies, while Tank, Grubby and I spent our time partying with the local chapter members with an eye to how they were running their chapter. We spent as much time as we could riding in the Black Hills of South Dakota, and I had some of the best times of my life riding in that part of the country.

There is a certain mystique about the Black Hills. The beautiful evergreen pines and the smell of the forest was hypnotizing. The old cowboy movies I watched as a kid replayed in my mind every time I rode there. I saw myself as a modern-day outlaw on a steel horse, riding in the footsteps of the outlaws who rode real horses there a hundred years before. At times, I would pull off on a trail and ride back into the forest until I could no longer see the road. I would walk around in the forest with the feeling that I was walking where no one had ever walked before.

South Dakota truly is the most beautiful state in the country, and it was no surprise to me that the sculptor Gutzon Borglum chose it when he set out to carve Mount Rushmore. The first time I saw it I was blown away. But the thing that really struck me was how he was able to accomplish what he did without any help from the federal government. Truly amazing.

At the same time, it was impossible for me not to be saddened by the plight of the Native Americans I saw in South Dakota. Having been born in the South, I knew of racism toward the blacks and Mexicans. I remember "colored only" drinking fountains, and shops and restaurants where the "colored" had to use the back door. However, what I saw and experienced in Rapid City was far more serious than I could ever have imagined when it came to treating others as an inferior species.

When we were not out riding and enjoying the scenery, we spent a lot of time at a small tin-shack motorcycle shop in Rapid City that was owned by a Bandido named Porky. I would hang around there for hours, helping him work on Harleys and learning even more from his wealth of knowledge. He now owns a state-of-the-art motorcycle shop there and specializes in Harley Davidson repair and high-performance engine building. I'm still friends with Porky today.

I began a love affair with the Black Hills in the short time I was in Rapid City. The roads always led to places of untamed raw beauty, where you could sometimes even see wild buffalo roaming the prairie.

In early May of 1973, Tank, Grubby, Shooter, Crowfoot, Sideways, Porky and I decided to take a trip to the eastern side of the state to Sioux Falls. Another Bandido chapter had just started up in this area and we decided it was time to check them out.

The ride across South Dakota was pleasant and uneventful. We took our time, enjoying the weather and looking out at the rolling meadows and flat treeless plains before stopping to relax at a bar in a little town called Lakota. I remember talking to some of the local men there and not receiving a very warm welcome. They acted as if we were there to take over their little town and have our way with the local women. Either they had watched too many biker flicks, or perhaps they were feeling a little guilt over their continuing poor treatment of the Native Americans who lived there. I never knew what their real problem was, but we didn't stay long enough to find out.

We rode on east and crossed the Columbia River, stopping at a park where I sat on a hill to take in the scenery, thinking this was the best ride I had been on in a long time. After smoking a joint or two, we continued on and finally arrived in Sioux Falls.

We met up with the brothers in the new chapter and began to party with them out in the country at a spot where we had a big campfire and some food waiting for us. There were also some hang-a-rounds from town who came out to party with us. One of these was a girl who decided to share her affections with a couple of the brothers. We all were having a good time drinking and smoking a little weed.

The party eventually moved back into town to a place called the J and M Tavern. We were not aware of it at the time, but an old enemy of one of the brothers was hatching a plan to get revenge. He was up for trial on a third felony charge and facing the possibility of life in prison on the habitual criminal statute.

Thinking the authorities would go easy on him when he came up for trial, he made a call to a detective in the police department and reported that the Bandidos were in town and he was going to go down to the tavern and start some trouble so the cops could arrest them. I don't know for sure, but apparently from what I heard, the cops he talked to thought this was a good idea.

When he arrived a little after midnight, the bar was smoky and crowded. What little light there was came mostly from the buzzing neon beer signs and the islands of light surrounding the pool tables. He approached us from the darkness, and as I turned my head, I saw him pull a gun from his waistband. There was a lot of shouting, and then I heard a shot. Naturally, I thought he had begun shooting.

My reaction was more instinct than anything else. The instinct of self-preservation, the strongest instinct of all, and in an instant that will live with me forever, I lunged at him with my knife and headed for the door.

As soon as I was outside, I jumped on my bike and fled. I managed to make it a few blocks before a police car pulled up beside me, and the cop inside was pointing a sawed-off shotgun right at me.

Looking down the barrel of that shotgun was like looking into a twelve-inch drainpipe, and the way he was leaning out his window and trying to balance himself on his elbows, it looked like I could just as easily have been shot by accident. "Pull over or I'll blow your ass off that bike!" he shouted.

Needless to say, I pulled over. The following day, I woke up in a cold jail cell, hungover, scared, and with only a vague memory of the events from the previous night. The only thing I knew for sure was that I was definitely in trouble.

CHAPTER 10

It took everything I had to keep my nerves under control when two detectives finally led me to an interrogation room. I was informed that the man I stabbed had died, and as it turned out, the shot I heard came from someone shooting the man in the head.

Naturally, the cops wanted to know who shot him. At the same time, they also pumped me for information on the Bandidos Motorcycle Club. Problem was, I really didn't remember, and even if I had, I wouldn't have told them anything out of a sense of loyalty to my brothers. In the noise and confusion and fear of the night before, it was all pretty much a blur. And that was the honest truth.

But the real stunner was still to come. Even though I had clearly acted in self-defense, I was being charged with the man's murder simply because they had my knife with his blood on it. Worse than that, these guys were charging me with premeditated murder in the first degree!

I never knew exactly where I had stabbed the man. In my mind, it was a superficial wound at best from a quick swipe while I was trying to get out the door. However, in the intelligent rationale from the police point of view, the knife wound I had inflicted caused the man to bleed out and die. They didn't seem to care much about the gunshot wound to his head. They also didn't seem to care that he had a gun and I was defending myself with a knife. They had a Bandido in custody, and that's the only thing that seemed to matter to them!

A few days later, I found myself talking to a local attorney. After telling him my side of the story, he agreed to take my case. After that, I made the hardest phone call I had ever made. The call to my parents. As I waited for them to answer, their warnings about my lifestyle echoed in my mind; "If you don't straighten up and fly right, you'll end up in prison". It seemed that I had finally fulfilled their prophecy. Thus began a three year legal battle financed by my father. A father who had never been arrested, never drank or done anything wrong in his life. A father who was now willing to sacrifice his life savings to keep me out of prison.

Eventually, after 76 days in the Minnehaha County Jail, I was bailed out on a forty-thousand-dollar cash bond that my father had taken from his life savings, where it sat in a safe in the Minnehaha County Courthouse for over three years. The money drew no interest for all that time and my father had to pay the lawyer fees out of it when the case was over.

During the time I spent in county jail, I attended several hearings to exclude evidence and have my bond reduced. The original charge was first degree murder for stabbing the man in the bar. I was also charged with rape and kidnap because the lady from the party was forced to file on several of us by her boyfriend who did not approve of her partying and sharing her affections with some of us.

Once the true facts came to light, the rape and kidnap charges were dropped and all my brothers who were arrested with me were released. I was the only one with the murder charge since mine was the only knife with his blood on the blade. My first bond was reduced to a quarter million, then reduced again to a hundred thousand before they finally settled on forty thousand cash.

There are some advantages to being in a small county jail and being a member of an outlaw motorcycle club. I was held in what was referred to as the felony tank. This is a row of four, two-man cells and a connected day room with a long table for meals and playing cards or dominoes.

We were allowed to stay in the day room anytime we wanted except after lights out. Due to my size and standing, I became the tank boss. We were given meals, medications and mail, plus we had a small commissary. Money for the commissary came from an old lady I had who was working in Rapid City.

If a new guy came into the tank and didn't follow the rules, it fell on me to show him who was boss. Most of the time the other guys would let a new guy know about the rules to save him from the pain and embarrassment of a beatdown. I was also in the tank longer than anyone else, so I assigned job duties to each man and made sure that their chores were done or else. I wasn't going to live in a dirty environment.

It was during this time in the felony tank that I met a man named Russell Means. Means was a leader in the American Indian Movement and was involved with the attack on Native Americans at Wounded Knee. He had been arrested and brought to Minnehaha County Jail on a suspicion of involvement with the killing of a federal agent.

I invited Means to share my cell since we were the oldest and probably the smartest guys in the tank at that time. We would sit and talk for hours at night about the plight of Native Americans and how much the government had persecuted them. I would draw correlations between his people and the outlaw bikers of my day and how we were also persecuted for wanting to be free instead of rubber stamp members of society.

We talked about how people feared what they didn't understand and how that fear allowed them to become victims of government propaganda. I also learned a lot about the importance of Native American traditions, like the wearing of long hair and not being able to cut it without permission from the elders. Because of their traditions, life behind bars was difficult for him. Native Americans believe in the circle of life, and it was hard to go into a building or room and leave by the same doorway.

I see him now and again in movies and on television, and I often wonder if he even remembers the time he spent talking to a big biker from Texas in that battleship gray cell.

The days were hot and the nights were long and a little bit cooler. I learned how to make a jailhouse cooler with running water in the faucet. I became adept at making candles from melted wax off drinking cups that we shaped by pouring it into cardboard toilet paper rolls. Three woven mop strings made for an efficient wick. The lights were turned off at 10 pm, so we would use the candles for reading and staying up late.

After my bond was reduced to forty thousand dollars cash, my father drove up to Sioux Falls and picked me up. My parents had also made the trip up there after I was arrested, but the authorities never allowed us to see each other without a cage or bars between us.

We picked up my bike from a brother in Sioux Falls who had gotten it out of the pound for me while I was in jail. We then loaded the bike into the back of my brother's Ford Ranchero and drove back across South Dakota to Rapid City to pick up Lynn and the rest of our meager belongings.

I can tell you that there were some long and lonely miles in that Ranchero. We didn't talk a great deal and spent most of our time tiptoeing around the elephant in the room. On the one hand, I was eaten up with a great deal of guilt for letting my family down like I had, but I also felt resentment for what I experienced growing up, feeling like my youth had been taken away from me.

It took us four days to make it back to Aransas Pass, Texas. Lynn and I moved into the trailer with my parents, but the fact that Lynn and I weren't married made it uncomfortable for my parents. We eventually moved back to Corpus Christi and lived with my old brother, Jerry, and his wife, Frenchie, before moving out to Flour Bluff to live on our own.

Thus began my three-and-a-half-year journey of living out on bond with a first-degree murder charge hanging over my head. I started doing some work for a brother in a shop he had opened up and Lynn started dancing again, which brought in the majority of our money.

Since I was bonded out to my father on a cash bond, I could move around where I wanted to as long as I could keep him thinking I wasn't doing anything that would get me into more trouble. But a leopard doesn't change his spots that easily, and I had re-united with my old school friend, William, who was into the marijuana smuggling business.

Short of cash, I soon began doing some work for him and delivering some loads to Mississippi and Tennessee. Sometime in the early part of 1975, Lynn moved out. I was still transporting marijuana up the country on a monthly basis, so I got a Pitbull named Butch to keep me company on my trips. I wore a big black cowboy hat, western shirts and cowboy boots for my cover, and always wore long sleeves to cover up my tattoos because I was still quite memorable in a crowd of people if they saw my artwork.

I also made a few trips to the Mexican border towns across the Rio Grande and delivered some firearms and night scopes to some connections there. I was really afraid on those trips, but the money always made it worth the risk for me.

Near the middle of 1975, I began working for a brother managing a titty bar in Corpus on the night shift. His 18 year old daughter had just come from California and had begun working for me. She was tall and blonde and had a gorgeous body, and she quickly became my old lady. Needless to say, she was a good money maker and she liked the protection I gave her. We stayed together for a few months, but eventually she wanted to be on her own and we split up. She continued to work for me and we are still friends to this day.

I had another girl working for me named Margie, who also became my old lady. She was olive-skinned with long brown hair, brown eyes and a beautiful body. She was a good money maker and didn't mind turning tricks for extra money. The problem was, she was also a needle user and a speed freak, and her paranoia was unbearable at times.

She would freak out if there was a car in our parking lot that she didn't recognize, and would spend hours going through the phone book looking for names of people she might know. One night she got really wired and began brushing and combing her hair so much that the comb got tangled up in it and we had to cut it out.

There were also countless nights when I would get calls from pimps and bar owners in town telling me to come and get her before they killed her for starting trouble. Even then, I stayed with her for the money she brought in. We had a nice apartment, furniture, TV, plus a state-of-the-art stereo system. It amazes me now that I put up with so much craziness just for money and material things.

It was around this time that I again began experiencing a great deal of pain in my lower back. I had already undergone back surgery in1971, but had gained weight and had continued riding rigid-frame Harleys. When I was arrested in Sioux Falls, I weighed around 275 pounds. By 1975, I was up to 290.

I began taking walks on the beach every day and started counting calories. I also made weekly trips to a chiropractor in Corpus Christi who had taken a personal interest in my weight program. Soon, I began losing weight and managed to lose a hundred pounds in eleven months, eventually getting down to one hundred and fifty-nine pounds. I wore size thirty-two pants and had finally achieved the physical body that I had dreamed of having all my life.

In spring the of 1976, I got a call from my lawyer in Sioux Falls. He told me to get a plane ticket and meet him in Chicago for a series of polygraph tests. We knew the results would be inadmissible as evidence in court, however they could be used to bolster my claim of self-defense to the prosecution.

 I never denied the fact that I stabbed the man in the bar. My fight was against the charge that the offense was premeditated first degree murder, an unreasonable charge that the prosecutor continued to pursue against me. After I arrived in Chicago, I took a long cab ride straight to my hotel. This was my first time in a big city with skyscrapers and I felt really small when I looked down from my window at all the people below. The next morning, I met up with my lawyer and spent most of the day undergoing nine different polygraph examinations and passing all of them.

Once I was back home, I continued to have severe back pain and was forced to undergo another surgery for the ruptured discs in my lower back. The surgery was done in the exact scar as my first surgery, but I still suffered intense pain in the same area. I was admitted back to the hospital and the doctor discovered that I had scar tissue from the previous surgery and had to undergo yet another surgery in the same place. I suggested to the doctor that he should just install a zipper to make it easier for him the next time.

CHAPTER 11

In November of 1976, I received a call from my lawyer in Sioux Falls. He told me that the prosecutor was willing to offer me a plea bargain. In a low monotone, he told me that instead of a possible life sentence for first degree murder, the prosecutor was willing to recommend a five-year sentence in the South Dakota State Penitentiary if I pled guilty to second degree manslaughter. I was silent for about a minute before I asked him what I should do. He said take the offer. The sound of his voice told me that after three-and-a-half years, he had finally gotten the ear of the judge and this was my best shot.

I told him I was ready to take the deal and he told me to be in court in Sioux Falls on November 29, 1976. My parents and I flew to Sioux Falls and arrived on the 28th. It was bitter cold and snow was on the ground the next morning when we arrived at the courthouse to meet with my lawyer. He explained that I would have a chance to plead my case to the judge and that my parents would also be able to testify in my defense. All of the other charges were not allowed to be mentioned and the prosecutor could only present the evidence he had for a second degree manslaughter charge instead of a murder charge.

After tearful testimony from my mother and a stoic and humble presentation from my father, I took the stand to repeat my claim of self-defense. The prosecutor then presented his evidence and asked the court to sentence me to five years.

In a moment I'll never forget, the judge called me to the bench and told me that he was turning me over to the custody of the South Dakota State Penitentiary for a time no longer than four years. He then suspended two years of that sentence and took off the 76 days I had spent in county jail in 1972. I was also informed that when I was processed into the penitentiary, I would be given four months of good time provided I didn't get into trouble while I was incarcerated. When the smoke cleared, I had a sentence of a little over 17 months. I knew then that my lawyer had definitely worked some kind of miracle on my behalf, and I'll always be eternally grateful to that man.

I was allowed to leave the courthouse for a final day of freedom, and the next day my father drove me past that line of leafless trees bordering the road that led up the hill to the state prison. My father had never been a man given to showing his emotions, and for the first time in my life, I saw tears in his eyes that day when he told me he loved me. I knew that I had let him and my mother down in the worst way ever, and it broke my heart to see how much I had hurt them. Before I walked away, he told me to do my time like a man and return home with my head held high. I promised him then and there I would change. A promise I intended to keep. But no matter how sincere we are, fate has a funny way of altering our promises, and unfortunately, it would intervene again.

Nothing can prepare a person for entering a maximum-security penitentiary. A sense of numbness overwhelmed me as I passed into the most surreal atmosphere I had ever encountered. It was as if the person who had been me began to vanish, and I became a number in a system.

After having me remove all my clothes, they gave me a thorough washdown with a delousing solution that smelled strongly of kerosene and some other unknown chemical. I was then issued the standard orange jumpsuit for all new "fish" in the system, along with a pair of black lace-up "state shoes" that didn't fit.

Wearing my new uniform, I was assigned a communal cell in the orientation and identification area known as the "fish tank". This was to be my home for the next week. I quickly learned that prisons are never quiet. Day area televisions are always at a high-volume level in order to be heard over a baseline noise level of loud inmate conversations mingled with intermittent shouts and the constant bangs and clangs from living in a metal environment. The noise level is even higher in the tiers where the cells are located.

I found out later that there is a method to this madness in the convict code. The guards become accustomed to the level of noise … a level of noise that is used as a tool for the convicts to hide their nefarious activities behind the scenes in the more isolated areas of the prison.

During my week in the fish tank, I underwent a cursory physical exam by a bored prison doctor. There were also sessions with counselors who actually showed more interest than most of the other professionals I saw.

I had a few sessions with a Dr Mueller, a quiet and unassuming man who showed an interest in my past. He put me through a complete psychological screening, including the long and seemingly pointless

Minnesota Multiple Personality Inventory, also known as the MMPI, plus a sit-down with some amusing Rorschach inkblot tests.

In our final session, I learned that my I.Q was 140 and that I had no real psychiatric problems. Most importantly of all, he let me know that he thought I didn't belong there. I told him to "Hold that thought!", because I believed his evaluation would be helpful at my first parole hearing coming up in a little over four months.

After a week in the fish tank, I was assigned to my "house", the term used by convicts when referring to their cell. My new address was the East Wing of the Second Tier, Number 76 E, of the South Dakota State Penitentiary, otherwise known as Granite City.

Inside my cell, my small bunk was attached to the wall, and there was a toilet and a sink with an unbreakable stainless-steel mirror. Because I had spent a great deal of my life working on boats in the Gulf of Mexico, I began to picture myself on a ship. The overheads of steel, the railings and steel stairs outside my cell, the steel walls that resembled bulkheads, all reminded me of being on a ship. I even referred to the communal dining room as the galley. I believe this small amount of familiarity brought me some degree of comfort.

The cell doors were opened all at once via a sliding mechanism controlled by a guard at the end of our cell block. I left my cell only to eat, spend time in the day room or yard, or go to appointments with doctors or prison officials. When the officials learned that I knew how to type, they decided to pay me eleven cents an hour to sit and type. They referred to this as clerical work and it was a form of rehabilitation, I suppose.

Returning to my cell is probably the cruelest memory I have. I had to shut the door on myself, reminding me every time I did it that it was my behaviors and choices that had brought me to this point.

Each cell had headphones that were tuned to local radio stations, so at least I could listen to music, news, weather and sports. I was finally able to watch television again when I bought a little TV from the Granite City Jaycees club, thus enabling me to escape the reality I was living. I spent a very lonely Christmas in my cell that year. The only saving grace was the T-bone steaks the cooks prepared for us. After eating, every convict was given a sack of Christmas candies and two pieces of fruit to take back to our cells.

The next week was New Year's Eve, and the prison was like a madhouse. Convicts from all five tiers threw stuff over the railings at midnight. Everything you could think of rained down on the bottom tier.

From bowls to burning pillows and anything that would make a noise or a mess.

The next morning, we all had to pitch in and clean up the floor, whether we had joined in the festivities or not. A great deal of that first month in general population was spent in the doctor's office. After my last back surgery, I still had a lot of lingering pain that extended down my left leg, and climbing the stairs to my tier only made it worse. I was taking Darvocet so regularly that I had built up a tolerance. My history of opiate use didn't help matters, so even though I was taking pain medication, I still felt no relief.

After giving my situation some thought, the medical staff decided I should be transferred to a more suitable location in order to provide time for me to heal properly. On a cold January day in 1977, with low gray clouds threatening snow, I was escorted down to the carpool area of the penitentiary. There, waiting for me, was Mr. Salem, the Warden. With no handcuffs or shackles, he had me crawl into the back of a black state station wagon with a pillow and a blanket, and drove me to the hospital in Yankton, South Dakota.

The warden and I became comfortable with each other almost immediately. He was a grandfatherly figure and was very affable and easy to talk to. We discussed the weather, family life, Bandido lifestyle, his experiences over the years working in the correctional field. All in all, we had a pleasant journey down to the state hospital.

Upon our arrival, I was taken to a private room and began to settle into my new surroundings. The pain in my back now extended down both legs and I was walking with a cane. My Darvocet dose was increased and I was encouraged to walk and move around more to prevent atrophy in my leg muscles. Swimming in a therapeutic pool was also added to my rehabilitation regimen, and I took full advantage of it every day I could.

At the end of my hall there was a day room with couches and chairs in front of a black and white TV. I would walk down there every night and watch television to indulge my passion for escapism. I was still incarcerated, but my escape pod from reality was right down the hall. I still watch a lot of television today, even though I'm no longer physically locked up, and am genuinely enthralled by reality shows. How unusual that I watch reality shows to escape from reality.

My time in the hospital was beneficial, but I was still in pain most of the time and my legs had experienced some atrophy in the hamstring muscles. In late February, I was transported back to prison in Sioux Falls in the same black station wagon. Upon my return, I was housed in a five-bed ward in the prison infirmary. Most of the time the beds would be occupied by inmates who were either too sick to be in general population or had been injured in fights with other inmates. I was the only permanent resident of the infirmary while I was there, and I was allowed to walk around in the halls whenever I felt like it.

One day, as I walked past a closed unmarked door, I decided to look inside. It was a storeroom of sorts, with desks, chairs and filing cabinets scattered around the room. I also noticed a bicycle exercise machine off in a corner. The next day, I asked the doctor if I could get permission to use the exercise machine to build the muscles up in my legs. He said I could use it any time I felt like it and I began a daily regimen of riding the exercise bike for thirty minutes.

About two weeks into my exercise routine, I was riding on the bicycle and looking around the room when I noticed four pieces of angle iron sticking up above the floor in the shape of a square. There were also some old power lines running down the back wall behind it.

Naturally, I became curious and asked the guard that evening what it was. He told me that the angle iron in the floor was where the electric chair had been bolted to the floor. The electric lines coming down the back wall had been attached to the chair to provide the lethal dose of electricity; however, they were no longer hot (thank goodness). I had been exercising in a room where an untold number of men had spent the last moments of their lives, and the guard enjoyed telling me that there were also a number of ghost stories attached to the room.

In the second week of April, 1977, a guard came into the infirmary to inform me that I was to go before the parole board the next day. Since I was a first offender, I was eligible for parole in the first quarter of my sentence. This calculated to about four and a half months of prison time. I was taken before the parole board in a wheelchair since I was still having lower back pain. The board asked me a few cursory questions and told me I would hear from them the next day. I went back to the infirmary, and early the next morning I received an envelope with a pink slip inside. I was to be paroled the next day and returned to serve out my parole under the Texas State Parole Service.

On April 15, 1977, I walked out of Granite City to return home to Aransas Pass, Texas. At that moment, I knew that my lawyer truly had performed a legal miracle. I also owe a debt of gratitude to the South Dakota judge and the parole board for seeing that I was acting in self-defense and that it was the gunshot to the head from someone else that had killed the man. I had never even heard of anyone serving only four and a half months for second degree manslaughter. To say that I felt like the luckiest guy on the planet would have been an understatement.

My father was there to pick me up and we flew back to Texas. It was a strange flight and the culmination of a long and strange journey with many new and fearful experiences. I would be on parole in the State of Texas until November of 1978, and I was still a full-fledged Nomad in the Bandidos motorcycle club. But once I was back in Texas, I was informed by my parole officer that if I flew my colors or continued my association with the Bandidos, my parole would be revoked and I would be returned to South Dakota to complete my original sentence.

I decided then that the best course of action would be to retire from a brotherhood I had given so much of my heart and soul to, and was allowed to retire as a member in good standing. I had proven myself to be a standup guy and never told anyone about who I thought might have fired the shot into the man's brain in Sioux Falls that night. I kept my oath of silence and did the time, and my loyalty to the club can never be questioned or disregarded.

In all the time I spent in jail fighting for my freedom in the court system, I never got a visit from any member of the club, nor was ever offered any financial or legal help. Today, I still see some of the old-timers from those days, and most of them have retired in good standing as well.

As for the new breed of Bandidos, some of them know me and know who I am, and they treat me with the respect I earned and deserve. I still have the colors tattooed on my back and will die with the Fat Mexican, but I cannot and will not return to the lifestyle.

I had also made a promise to my parents that I would never go back to that lifestyle, and I still honor that promise today even though they are both deceased.

CHAPTER 12

Now that I was back in Texas and no longer a Bandido, I had no idea what I was going to do with my life. At the age of 32, I had no marketable skills to think of. I was a convicted felon with a prison record, no savings, and I had no real belongings except for the clothes on my back. And to add insult to injury, I had sold my motorcycle before I went to prison, so I didn't even have a bike to ride at the time.

The thought of assimilating back into the pre-Bandido society I had run away from was even more frightening than the thought of prison had been. My father had retired from dredge boat work and owned a little gas station in my hometown of Aransas Pass, where he and my brother were struggling to make a living for themselves.

Margie was still my old lady and had been living in our old apartment in Corpus Christi while I was in prison. I moved back in with her and let her support me with her dancing and turning tricks after hours, but while I had been gone, her drug addiction to speed had only gotten worse. She was constantly causing trouble with all the bar owners, stealing from tricks, and bringing more heat down around me than I needed, especially since I was on parole.

I finally told her that she could keep all the stuff we had accumulated together, including a car I had bought for her before I went to prison. All I wanted was out of the relationship. We parted ways and I moved back to Aransas to live with my parents. My father let me work at the gas station, but I wasn't paid very much since they were also providing my room and board.

One day I was working at the gas station when my old high school friend, William showed up. We began talking and he told me to come see him. The suggestion was that, if I worked for him, I could make some real money.

I also hooked up with J.T. Marshall, my old high school friend who had bought a bar on the outskirts of town. He taught me how to do the books and paid me a little wage under the table, plus I could drink for free any time I wanted.

I was living at home and finally making some money. Truth is, my drug addiction had never really ceased while I was in prison because of my back pain, and now that I was out, I began to do even more drugs. I was taking up to fifteen Darvocets every day for my back pain. These were prescription meds, but I would also do any street drugs I could find to numb the pain. I had all the marijuana I wanted due to my connection with William, and all the alcohol I wanted from the bar job.

I know that part of my extensive drug use was a result of my involvement with the death of the man in South Dakota. I became convinced that I was not a good person and never would be. I could never find forgiveness anywhere for what I had done with my life, and every time I made an attempt to do something good or noble, I would end up sabotaging myself. Drugs had always been a big part of my adult life, but at this juncture, they became the primary focus of my life.

Meanwhile, my friend William had built a metal building on the docks in Aransas Pass and fitted it with all the accoutrements of a shipbuilding enterprise. He had also bought a couple of shrimp boats, an oilfield supply boat, and a high-speed crew boat. In actuality, it was all a front he had set up to disguise a large smuggling enterprise he had started.

Together with my old Bandido brother Jerry, we would show up every morning to make the place look busy. We both received hourly wages to make things look legal and above board, while at the same time our boats were sailing off to Colombia and returning with thousands of pounds of marijuana.

They would return to little obscure bayous and harbors where William had paid off the owners and caretakers to look the other way while the boats were unloaded onto waiting 18-wheeler trucks. After they were loaded, they would be sealed with stolen or counterfeit seals and would scatter like cockroaches to places like Michigan, Illinois, Indiana, Tennessee or wherever a buyer was waiting. In those days, it was mostly enterprising Americans who were involved in drug smuggling. Nowadays, thanks in large part to the so-called war on drugs and a lax border policy, the Mexican drug cartels are in charge and entrenched all over our country.

After unloading, the boats would then return to the docks in Aransas Pass and Jerry and I would clean all traces of the previous voyage and make them ready for the next trip. At first, I still lived at my parents' house, but the hours got so hectic and I was in such demand to help with the unloading, that I began to live on one of the boats at the

52

shipyard. I had a little TV and central air in my own private captain's quarters, and the similarities of my time in the general population of South Dakota State Penitentiary and my life working on boats wasn't lost on me.

I also had free reign to smoke all the marijuana and do any other drugs I cared to do. Not to mention there was no rent to pay and William made sure the boat was always stocked with plenty of food. J.T. had been married to a girl named Diane, and she was still around as a part of his life because of their daughter Michele. Diane was an alcoholic and I was an addict, so naturally we became good friends. So good, in fact, that we eventually began dating each other. She had been divorced from J.T. for some time and he wasn't upset by our relationship. In February of 1978, Diane and I got married at a judge's office in Corpus Christi.

Just before our marriage, I had helped William with the unloading of one of the boats in the Victoria barge canal about 60 miles north of Aransas Pass. On that cold and misty January night, I was stationed next to a motorhome parked up on the levee from the docks where the boat was being unloaded. Inside was a man from Michigan who had a spectroscope and was able to monitor all the police and law enforcement agency radio broadcasts in that vicinity.

The dock owner had been paid handsomely in advance of the arrival of the shipment and I was armed with a high-powered rifle and a night scope. I was in constant radio contact with the men in the trucks and with men on the ground, and was the first line of defense against any hostile attacks by rival smugglers.

I guess William counted on me to pull the trigger since everyone knew I had already proven that I was willing to kill for a brother. I remember lying outside the motorhome, cold, wet and shivering in my long johns, thick camo coat and rain gear. I prayed to my "let's make a deal God" that, if He would only get me through this night alive without having to pull the trigger on anyone, that I would never agree to do anything like this again.

Fortunately, the unloading went off without a hitch, the trucks were loaded in record time and the boat returned to the dock while the rest of us returned to Aransas and celebrated a successful venture in the world of international drug smuggling. I was later handed a brown paper bag containing twelve thousand dollars in cash for my services that night.

Thanks to this infusion of cash, my new marriage turned into a whirlwind of spending. I bought wedding rings, paid for Diane to have a breast job, paid off her car and bought new furniture and carpet for our rented house in Aransas Pass.

While I continued working at the shipyard, I was still receiving visits from my parole officer on an intermittent basis. Luckily, I wasn't required to take a urinalysis drug test for the parole board because my charge wasn't drug related, and the use of drug tests wasn't as prevalent as it is today.

My parole officer would always call ahead and tell me the exact day and time for our visit and never stayed longer than fifteen minutes. I completed my probation in May of 1978 and received a document stating that my rights as a citizen had been returned, but that I was still prohibited from owning a firearm or ammunition. Strangely, the ownership of shotguns was not prohibited.

As mentioned before, Diane was an alcoholic and she continued to drink and go out with her female friends whenever she felt like it. I smoked weed every day and still took a lot of painkillers. Needless to say, our paths in marriage began to divert and we spent less and less time together. Eventually, her drinking and staying out got to be too much for me and I moved out to a little ranch that William had bought between Aransas Pass and Rockport, Texas.

In early August of 1978, I hired a lawyer who was an old friend of mine in Aransas Pass and had my marriage to Diane annulled. I was now a 33-year-old ex-convict with two marriages under my belt and living on my own again. The ranch I had moved to was part of a multi-acre site William had purchased with the intent of splitting it up and selling lots for a housing development.

The main house had two bedrooms, one bath, a large living room and kitchen with window air conditioning units. In addition to the main house, there was a large barn and a corral with a big tree growing in the middle.

William and another friend of ours who was a connoisseur of fine marijuana had planted several plants in the shelter of the big tree in the corral. Through our joint (no pun intended) efforts in cultivation, these plants produced some potent and very powerful buds that kept us well supplied for months. We never sold it, but needless to say we always had a few visitors at the ranch for obvious reasons.

There were barbecues at the ranch almost every weekend that included people from William's organization, and since the ranch was outside the city limits, we did some skeet shooting and practiced with shotguns for hours on end.

A portion of the ranch contained a freshwater reservoir filled from a well system that had been used to water livestock when the property was a working ranch. About four miles down the road from us, there was a tourist attraction called the Alligator Farm, where another friend of ours kept dozens of alligators. His nickname was, of course, Gator, and he charged people to watch him put on a show with his gators.

At some point in time, probably during Hurricane Celia in 1970, one of the alligators had made his way over to the ranch to take up residency in the reservoir. We started calling him "Boots". We would slap the water while calling his name, and after a few minutes he would surface with just his eyes and snout poking up out of the water as he swam toward us.

We would feed him whole chickens from the store, and after some of us went deer hunting, the carcasses always went to Boots. He was an amazing disposal system, and needless to say, no one ever went swimming in the reservoir.

At the time, I had an old Ford truck that I drove to the shipyard every day. I had not owned a motorcycle since I left for prison, and I was really missing the wind in my face and the freedom of riding a Harley. William was always buying cars and trucks, and I think he knew I missed it, so he bought a Harley Super Glide and told me to take care of it as if it were my own.

I was thrilled. I had a bike again. I couldn't ride with the Bandidos anymore, but I could still ride, and I quickly began making up for lost time. I would take rides by myself and go wherever I wanted to. I never had a lot of money, but William always made sure I had enough. I also had access to several of his cars as well as the huge self-contained motorhome we used as a lookout on several occasions.

I still continued to take a lot of Darvocet for my back pain, but I shied away from using any heroin or any strong opiates at that time because William didn't want a bunch of junkies working for him. Besides, we were all friends and William always kept us supplied with all the fine weed we wanted, and made sure we always had some money. There was always food and drink at the ranch house, I had no rent or bills to pay, and I had access to a Harley and several other vehicles. To say that William was a good friend is an understatement. He was one of the best friends I ever had.

Most of the time I lived at the ranch alone, but sometimes other guys we grew up with in Aransas Pass would stay there as well. William had already figured out that he could only trust people from his past … people he had known for a good part of their lives … something the

Mafia had also figured out years ago. We might have been smuggling weed, but mostly we were just South Texas boys who wanted to have fun and get high. But we also wanted to make money, and we were willing to take some extremely big risks to get it.

William saw the loyalty I had given to my Bandido brothers, and he made a place for me in an organization where that kind of loyalty would be appreciated. He also knew that I had already killed because of that same kind of loyalty, just like any good soldier would do, and that if it ever became necessary, he would be able to call on me to cross that line quicker than anyone else in the organization. I was also able to speak Spanish and had an uncanny ability not to show emotions in tight situations, all traits he knew he would need in me someday.

CHAPTER 13

At the end of 1978 and into 1979, I continued living at the ranch and working at the shipyard. My parents were still living in Aransas Pass and I would go by and see them occasionally. After the annulment with Diane, I didn't see them as often as I did when I was living in town with her. They never had a clue as to what was going on out at the ranch or at the harbor. Whether I was a member of an outlaw motorcycle club or involved in an international drug smuggling operation, it seemed as though I was always living a double life with them.

In February, William came out to the ranch and told me he had a job for me. He gave me a hotel key with a room number and told me to dress in my nicest clothes and drive one of his Mercedes up to the Houston Airport Hilton. Once there, I was to go up to the room where I would find two large suitcases. I was instructed to load the suitcases into the Mercedes and drive right back to the ranch the same day. I was not to speed or break any traffic laws or draw any attention to myself.

Early the next morning, I dressed in my only suit and headed for Houston in the Mercedes. The day was cold and clear with little traffic and I made good time, even driving the speed limit.

At the hotel, I parked and calmly walked through the front entrance wearing my Ray Ban sunglasses and took an elevator up to the room. Once I opened the door, it was obvious no one was there. In fact, it looked like no one had even stayed there. But on the bed, there were two large suitcases.

Both suitcases were extremely heavy, but I managed to carry them both to the elevator and out through the lobby. As soon as they were safely tucked away in the trunk of the Mercedes, I headed back down to South Texas. William had never told me what was in the bags. I suspected drugs of some kind. However, I had been around large quantities of marijuana in the past and the odor was hard to conceal. I could detect no scent from these bags.

William had also told me not to call him on the way back since he was always paranoid about phone conversations. This was in an era before cell phones, so all our calls were made on pay phones. We always carried rolls of quarters for pay phones back then, and he had set up elaborate code systems and trigger words to let me know what phone to call and at what time.

On the way back to Aransas Pass, I drove the exact speed limit and obeyed all traffic laws. When I arrived back at the ranch that afternoon, I was greeted by the sight of William's Mercedes in the driveway. Inside the house, he was smoking weed and waiting for me.

Together we unloaded the suitcases and carried them into the back bedroom of the house. While he produced the keys for the locks, I held my breath wondering what I had been carrying for the last 225 miles.

As soon as he opened the first suitcase, I let out a low whistle. The suitcase was stuffed with the most powerful drug of all. Money! The suitcases were filled with cash totaling two million dollars. I never realized how heavy that much money could be. I had been in possession of two million dollars for the last five hours and didn't even know it. Somehow, I believe that was part of the plan, and William paid me two thousand five hundred dollars for my services.

I was instructed to go to work the next morning and leave the suitcases in the closet because he didn't want anything to look out of the ordinary. We stayed up most of the night smoking weed, drinking and talking about the business. The next day I got up and William was gone. But the suitcases were still where we had left them and I never opened them again to look at the money.

I am a very loyal person and when someone puts their trust in me, I never betray that trust. William had seen that trait in me for years and knew he could always count on me to keep the business to myself. As instructed, I drove my old truck down to the shipyard and worked at looking busy as if it were just another regular day.

That evening, I returned to the ranch and the suitcases were gone. I figured William had got them and they were no longer any of my business. The next day, William came by the shipyard and called me into the office. He began asking me about the suitcases and the last time I saw them. He also asked if I had opened them and looked inside. I told him the only time I looked inside was the day before when he had opened them with his keys.

When I asked why, he calmly told me that someone had gotten onto the ranch and had stolen a few hundred thousand dollars out of one of the suitcases. It was not discovered until William had taken the suitcases somewhere else for a final count and to pay some outstanding debts with others in the business.

I assured him that I had not taken any money or even touched the suitcases after we put them in the closet. I'm well aware that the drug business is a dirty and unscrupulous world. William undoubtedly had some suspicions, but he told me that he had utmost trust in me and knew that I would never steal from him when all I had to do was ask and he would give me anything I wanted.

However, those he did business with weren't as trusting. I was the first person on their list of suspects, and they "asked" me to submit to a voice stress test. The next day, a man showed up and asked me some questions while taping our conversation.

Now remember, I had already undergone nine polygraph tests in Chicago in 1976, so I was not intimidated or rattled by any of this. Long story short, I calmly answered his questions and was found to be truthful, thereby allaying their suspicions of me.

When I think back on that incident, I am reminded that an addict will steal your stuff and then help you look for it. I sometimes wonder if William ever took one of those voice stress tests. After all, he was the only other person who knew about the two million dollars in the closet. If there really was a thief, there's little doubt in my mind that he or she would have taken the entire two million.

CHAPTER 14

I continued to live my double life out at the ranch, going to work every day in an effort to maintain our front at the shipyard. It was kind of an idyllic life. I would go to Corpus on the weekends to party at the local bars and meet women. I was the elusive, hard-to-figure-out guy who drove a different car every day and had lots of cash with no visible means of support.

I was still in pretty good physical shape at the time, with long salt and pepper hair and a salt and pepper beard. These were my Kris Kristofferson days. I was told I looked like him and I rode that horse for as long as possible. My relationships with women at the time never lasted very long because I wasn't interested in anything permanent. I was having fun and didn't want the hedonistic lifestyle to stop. In my other life, I still took dangerous risks transporting marijuana or guns or money for William. I rode the Harley any time I wanted and the rent was free.

Around this time, I began going over to Port Aransas to visit friends from my younger days. There were two brothers named Tom and Pat that I ran around with back in my high school days. Tom owned the same bar where some of my Bandido brothers were about to become involved in a huge fight before my cop friend John Lyman showed up and things calmed down.

I enjoyed a lot of respect because of my days as a Bandido and the fact that I had gone to prison for manslaughter. The fact that I had money most of the time and drove a lot of different vehicles was a status symbol. Naturally, I continued picking up girls in bars, but these brief encounters were never meaningful until I met a girl named Sheri.

Sheri was only 17 and I was 34 at the time. However, she had been legally declared an adult due to a marriage that was ending. The moment we met, there was a mutual attraction and I began staying with her at her house on the island.

She turned 18 that summer, and by then I had rented a little cottage on the island. We called it the square donut because of the strange layout. It was basically one room with a little kitchen and living area on one side, a bath at the back, and the bed to the right of the front door. Because

Port Aransas was a tourist town, these kinds of self-contained cottages were all over the island.

I still continued working at the shipyard in Aransas Pass and began riding the Harley more and more with old and new friends. We called ourselves the "Loosely Formed Non-Existent Organization of Unorganized Bikers". Besides Sheri and I, this little group consisted of Corky and his wife Tommie, Boxcar and Sherry, Vinton and Sweet Mary, Ronnie and Melissa, and George and Leah.

Together we explored the coastal flatlands of South Texas, but after living on an island surrounded by salt water, we longed for freshwater lakes, clear rivers to swim in, and hills with curving back roads to ride our bikes on. In late September of 1979, we made reservations at the Cold Springs Campground on the Frio River. The members of the L F N E O U B loaded a trailer with tents, camping gear, food and plenty of beer and we headed off for a four-day vacation in the Texas Hill Country.

There's an irony in that people from the coast want to vacation inland, and those who live inland hightail it for the beach the first chance they get. For me, our little run to the Hill Country reminded me of the Bandido lifestyle, riding in a pack of friends and enjoying a way of life most people never experience.

We spent that long weekend reveling in the change of scenery and the break from the humidity of the coast. We stayed up late, partying around a huge campfire and eating grilled steaks and burgers. Our cabins were air conditioned and there was no television or phone. We slept late, and during the days we would swim or lay out on the banks of the cool Frio River, smoking weed and drinking beer under the overhanging cypress trees.

We even took turns swinging out over the clear water on a rope swing, splashing into the river only to climb out and repeat the thrill again. For many of us, this was a return to the summer days of childhood, free from the cares of the world.

On the third day, we woke up early and had a hearty breakfast of homemade tacos and coffee. After smoking a couple of joints, we mounted our bikes and headed for the little river town of Leakey to ride the infamous ranch roads known as the Twisted Sisters, some of the gnarliest and most exciting motorcycle riding roads in Texas.

Today, there's a sign posted at the city limits on Ranch Road 335 reminding riders that, since 2006, thirteen riders have lost their lives in motorcycle related accidents on the twisting road ahead. Only a fool would fail to heed a warning like that.

On our last day, we loaded up and headed back to the island. Even though we had enjoyed our time away, we had been gone just long enough to start missing the sight of the ocean and the sound of seagulls singing overhead. We were sad that our trip was over, but we were returning to our own little piece of paradise, and best of all, we were riding motorcycles.

Back home, I returned to my routine of smoking weed and working at the shipyard for William. Boats would return and we would perform the needed repairs and give them a thorough cleaning to remove any traces of marijuana after they were unloaded. My old Bandido friend Jerry was also an accomplished welder, and we spent days fabricating secret compartments to hide the loads coming in from Colombia.

Sometimes we got creative, building clever containers that looked like legitimate equipment. We once constructed some huge metal containers designed to look like the kind of spools that held long steel cable seen around every shipyard. We would build them at the shop in Aransas Pass and load them onto trucks for shipment to various locations undisclosed to me or anyone else at the shop. Just like the CIA, everything was on a need-to-know basis.

I was being paid six dollars hourly by William's company in the form of a regular paycheck in case anyone checked. But most of my money came directly from William in the form of cash whenever I asked for it. But it was never enough.

At times I felt like I was being strung along, chasing the proverbial carrot at the end of a stick. I was envious of his Mercedes and fancy motorhomes, along with the carefree lifestyle accented by his frivolous spending and constant displays of large wads of cash. But now that I look back on it, I had a somewhat carefree lifestyle of my own. I had a motorcycle to ride and all the high-grade marijuana I wanted to smoke. The addictive part of my character had a hold on me, even though I was not fully aware of the power it already had on my life.

It was at this time that William came by the shop and we began talking about how I could make some more money. Conn Brown Harbor in Aransas Pass had been the home of the largest shrimp boat fleet in the country since the 1930s. That said, the 1970s were probably the most productive years in its history, and William had an acquaintance there who controlled the entire inventory in a local shrimp packing plant.

This one plant was where hundreds of boats unloaded and sold their catch. After the shrimp was unloaded, it was taken to a nearby freezer plant where the catch was sized according to the number of shrimps per pound, then packed in five-pound packages before being quick-frozen. These packages in turn were boxed in 50-pound lots and stored in giant zero-degree vaults until they were sold wholesale and loaded into trucks for distribution all over the world.

Shrimp are priced according to size. Shrimp in the 26-30 range per pound are small and cost less, whereas shrimp in the 10-16 range is much larger and sold at a much higher price. I would call the main offices and get a quote for a fifty-pound box of 26-30 shrimp and order two boxes. That night, I would call our friend and tell him what I had ordered and place an order with him off the books for three more boxes of the much larger shrimp for one hundred dollars per box.

The next day, our friend would strategically place boxes around the very last bay to prevent the purchasing clerk from having a clear line of sight of the area. I would back my truck up to the bay and leave a Marlboro pack with the correct amount of money for our deal inside of the pack, then go upstairs and get the invoice for the boxes that I had ordered the previous day from the main office. Invoice in hand, I would go back downstairs to the purchasing clerk's window and pay her in cash for the invoiced boxes.

I would then take the receipt to our friend and wait beside my truck. I would always notice that the Marlboro box was gone before he came blasting through the freezer's hanging plastic barriers and begin throwing boxes into the back of my truck. I hastily covered them with a tarp and made my way to the gate, where I calmly handed the gate guard a copy of my receipt before driving away with three extra fifty-pound boxes of very expensive shrimp.

Once I made it back to the island, I would break all the boxes open and dump the frozen shrimp into large Igloo ice chests and pack them with enough ice to keep them cold. I already had a friend on the island who was selling shrimp on the side of the road to tourists, and we partnered up. Our deal was always better because the tourists got more shrimp for a cheaper price. Additionally, a couple of friends were gill netting at night and we started selling fresh fish as well. Once word got out, this turned into a very lucrative enterprise.

I was able to trade my old pickup in for a new Ford Econoline van my father co-signed for. My partner bought a pickup and we got a good deal on a walk-in freezer to store all of our ice and shrimp. We then hired a couple of local girls to sell shrimp for us. Needless to say, business was great. I used my new van to haul our fresh fish and shrimp to a restaurant in San Antonio and began selling by the side of the road there too.

We would sell at crossroads and service station parking lots all over San Antonio. I had friends there from my years in the Bandidos and began making deliveries of high-grade weed there as well to trusted people and associates while I was selling shrimp and fish. On the outside, the entire enterprise was legal. We had all the appropriate fish and game licenses, our scales were calibrated and inspected, health regulations were all met, and our business licenses were up to date. We had a good thing going, and it got us through the winter of 1979.

By now, Sheri and I were living in a community of little tourist cottages that had been built with little or no insulation back in the 1930's. My old friends, Tommy and Pat, had inherited them from their parents, who had been some of the early settlers on the island. I remember the beds always having a fine coat of sand on them. For anyone who lives in Port Aransas, sand becomes a way of life.

In time, they began renting them out to locals and friends they had known over the years, and the nine cottages became a tight knit community of free-spirited and fun-loving islanders. Times were good, but they had the potential for getting better.

CHAPTER 15

In November, William approached me with a proposition to make some serious money. The first thing he wanted me to do was apply for a passport. I wasn't really sure I would be able to acquire one with my record as a convicted felon, but as it turned out, it wasn't a problem since I had completed the terms of my parole and had my rights restored. A few weeks after I submitted the paperwork, I had my passport.

In the last week of December, I kissed Sheri goodbye and William and I flew to Houston, where we bought round trip tickets to Panama City, Panama. International travel was easy and inexpensive in those days, and purchasing tickets with cash was an everyday occurrence. However, when you fly into another country, you're required to purchase a round trip ticket.

Even though we were flying to Panama, our ultimate destination was Colombia, so we purchased our tickets to Bogota in Panama so as not to draw suspicion when leaving and returning to the United States. We flew first class and, as usual, every trip with William was a party. He was wearing a Rolex and 24 karat gold Thai neck and wrist jewelry. We were dressed as wealthy Texans going to Panama to gamble, drink and chase the women.

After landing in Panama City, we were easily passed through customs and immigration after they glanced inside our bags and stamped our passports. In case they asked, our cover for employment was construction and design of vessels since William owned a boat company and I worked for him.

Panama is a country of lush jungles, a tropical climate, and beaches on the Caribbean Sea and North Pacific Ocean. Verdant colors and tropical flowers were everywhere. So was the heat. Luckily, we had air-conditioned rooms in the downtown high-rise Holiday Inn Hotel overlooking the Pacific Ocean. I remember that one of the balconies of a nearby high rise had a huge ornate metal cage housing some beautiful red, green and blue macaws. The racket those parrots made could be heard for blocks. I was slightly amazed when the owners suddenly released them to soar among the high-rise buildings before returning to their cages voluntarily after a few hours of free wing time.

The long boulevard along the shore was populated by vendors selling souvenirs, and after strolling along the promenade and eating some fresh ceviche from a pushcart, I bought Sheri a white sleeveless dress that I planned to give her when I returned to Texas.

In order to maintain our cover as tourists, we visited markets and tourist attractions in the city, and I was introduced to my first experience in a casino. You would think that as a former Bandido, I would have been a little more worldly, but in truth, I was slightly intimidated by the slot machines, blackjack tables and roulette wheels. I was 34 years old and had never set foot in one of these establishments. I certainly was not familiar with the rules of the games and was overwhelmed by the amounts of money I saw on the tables.

I played some slot machines while William was throwing money around and playing all the games. He gave me some money to gamble, but I ended up keeping most of it. We both availed ourselves of the free drinks and got pretty wasted before the night was over.

During our travels around the city, William would make stops at the major banking institutions to move money around from different accounts in Panama and his offshore accounts in Grand Cayman. We left the States with a few hundred dollars because it is illegal to leave the country with more than ten thousand dollars without declaring it and explaining why you were carrying so much. We didn't want to draw any suspicion to ourselves, and any money we needed after we arrived in Panama could easily be obtained with another series of transfers.

During our stay in Panama, I was introduced to one of William's connections, a man named Sonny. He was a Colombian national and had a home in Panama. Sonny would later prove to be my best friend and traveling companion after we left Panama and flew to Colombia. He was a short, thin man with a light complexion, hawk-like nose and black hair. His long fingers and meticulous grooming made him look almost effeminate, but I didn't think he was gay, especially when I found out he had a girlfriend in Panama and another in Colombia.

Sonny spoke Spanish as well as fluent English, which was one of the reasons he later proved to be my best friend. His translation skills and knowledge of different local dialects probably saved my life on more than one occasion.

William had reserved a room for him at our hotel and Sonny accompanied us wherever we went from this day forward. Over the next few days, we traveled around the city, tying up loose ends before we flew on to our real destination, Bogota, Colombia.

Each of us was able to conceal fifteen thousand dollars cash on ourselves for the last jump to Colombia. We carried money in our shoes, taped around our ankles, and in money belts with hidden compartments. We also bought cases of Ray Ban sunglasses and Buck knives after being advised that these prized items would be excellent for bribing guards and officials as we traveled the highways and back roads of Colombia.

Our departure from the airport in Panama City was smooth as silk, and on New Year's Eve of 1980, we landed in Bogota, Colombia, where we would spend the next unforgettable fifty days in that beautiful but terrifying country.

Colombia is a third-world country in almost every sense. With abject poverty and a small middle class, the majority of the country's wealth is controlled by a small percentage at the top of the pecking order. Like so many South and Central American countries, the rich got richer while the poor continued to get very little, and it was this dynamic that fueled the rise in narcotics trafficking in this part of the world.

At the airport, the atmosphere is one of confused chaos filled with frustrated international travelers waiting in long lines at ticket counters. The overhead announcements are made in either rapid-fire Spanish or in heavily accented attempts at English over speaker systems that were always scratchy sounding.

Sonny had warned us about the presence of professional pickpockets and thieves who would snatch jewelry from our necks, or use straight razors to cut the shoulder straps of our carry-on bags as they casually strolled by. He also told us to remain close to each other, and if we had an extra bag, we should keep a foot on it to discourage thieves.

Customs and immigration came with its own set of rules and frustrations. Gone is the laughter and excitement that accompanies most arrivals in exotic new countries after tourists notice the overwhelming presence of Colombian soldiers armed with Uzis, M16s and AK47s.

In Columbia, more than anywhere else except maybe El Salvador and Honduras, travelers from the US are quickly introduced to the reality of how things work under a corrupt and oppressive regime. A bag that catches an inspector's eye can be spirited away to an unknown location for further inspection while you are detained. After the bag is returned, there is usually an exhausting questioning session meant to intimidate you before you're released, only to discover later that a few items have mysteriously disappeared from your luggage.

67

The immigration window can be another challenge. Foreign officials seem to take a sadistic joy in scrutinizing you with their beady questioning eyes. There could be a few simple questions about the reason for your visit, or you could receive the fifth degree, questioning you about your picture and why it doesn't look like you, regardless of the fact that it might be ten years old. The number of stamps from different countries can also lead to other questions as to why you needed to visit so many other countries. The possibilities for official bullying are endless.

Luckily for us, we never had to endure the intimidating nonsense at the airport that most travelers experienced. Waiting for us was a tall immaculately-groomed man wearing an expensive three-piece Italian suit who carried himself with the grace of a professional athlete. Speaking in heavily accented English, he told us his name was Arnulfo and welcomed us to Colombia.

Arnulfo was a member of the DAS, the Administrative Department of Security in Colombia responsible for immigration. The DAS has been widely compared to our CIA and is also known to work with the National Police as well as the DEA in the US.

While other travelers queued up for customs, Arnulfo had magically bestowed diplomatic status on us and we passed through customs without a single question or suspicious look. Thanks to our new Columbian friend, we were now safely in Bogota, our jumping off point for travel farther into the country.

Bogota is a city of eight million people and lies eight thousand feet above sea level on a high plateau in the Andes Mountains. The city itself sits in a bowl surrounded by those mountains, and the temperature is generally on the cool side. The rainy season brings the temperatures down even more, and the nights can be downright cold.

Driving through the city, our olfactory senses were overwhelmed by diesel fumes. Nearly every vehicle in the city is powered by diesel engines, and the fumes that linger between the mountains can be suffocating at times.

The presence of armed guards was commonplace in the Capital District and the more affluent neighborhoods. Those areas were usually clean and well maintained, while the roads and streets in the poorer sections of the city were piled high with litter and the detritus of a swelling population.

Led by Arnulfo, we arrived at the Hotel Tequendama, an elegant high-rise hotel in the Financial District frequented by visiting businessmen. Arnulfo made all the arrangements with hotel management while we waited in the bar, and after a few complimentary drinks, we were escorted up to a lavish three-bedroom, three-bath suite with a breathtaking view of the city.

After unpacking our luggage in our respective rooms, we gathered in the living room to relax and get to know Arnulfo. When he removed his suit coat, I noticed that he was armed with two handguns in shoulder holsters worn under each arm. I asked him why he was carrying two weapons and he replied, "I have two hands" and smiled broadly.

This was an introduction for me into the not-so-subtle dangers of Colombia and the people who were now in charge of my safety. After all the cordialities, we got down to the business at hand. The first order of business was to lay all the smuggled cash out on the table as a down payment to Arnulfo for our future safety. Especially mine.

After replenishing our coffers from the Columbian branch offices of the same cooperative banking institutions found in Panama, we spent a couple of days sightseeing in Bogota while travel arrangements for me and Sonny were being made by William.

We acted like tourists, using taxis to explore the city and buying souvenirs for our cover. We also went to bars and casinos. I remember one casino where a single bottle of Chivas Regal cost ninety dollars American. We probably drank a couple of bottles for sure. We were always able to find good weed, and of course cocaine was available wherever we went.

Bogota night life was in full disco swing in January of 1980. The clubs were called "discotecas", and the high-class Colombian and tourist partiers danced to the sounds of Kool and the Gang and ABBA all night long.

One afternoon, I asked a taxi driver if he knew where the Harley-Davidson shop was. He assured me that he could find the place and off we went. After a half hour of driving through the busy streets in the commercial section of the city, he pulled up to a little shop with a Harley-Davidson sign over a window and told me that this was the place I was looking for.

Inside, there was a little counter and pictures of motorcycles, but no motorcycles. I asked the young man behind the counter if he had any bikes for sale and he said that they would have to order one for me. He showed me to a small room stocked with oil, filters, a few parts and accessories, and announced that this was his entire inventory. Obviously, the Harley craze had not quite reached South America in 1980.

However, the night life and sightseeing were only temporary diversions because twenty-four hours later, I would be leaving Bogota for the real reason I was there.

CHAPTER 16

The next morning, William announced that he had made all the arrangements for Sonny and I to fly out of Bogota to the city of Barranquilla on the Caribbean coast. He handed us a pair of Avianca Airline tickets plus fifteen thousand dollars cash to keep our Colombian friends satisfied, and to cover our living expenses while we were under their care.

You see, after William returned to the States, I had agreed to stay in Colombia as a hostage of sorts to ensure that the weed we were purchasing arrived in the U.S. safely, and that the balance of the payment for the load would be paid in full to the Colombian cartel.

In other words, I was the guarantee of payment and would remain in Columbia as a guest of the cartel until they had their money. This was not an unusual business practice when it came to illegal drug transactions in those days, and I was not at all worried about William holding up his end of the bargain. We had been lifelong friends, and I knew that he would never leave me behind or let anything happen to me.

This was just the way business was done, and lifelong trusts were built between our two cultures. This kind of trust-building exercise was common among themselves, but they had to push the envelope to see if the trust was reciprocal when it came to dealing with their foreign partners. With these guys, you had to earn their respect, and after a lifetime of gaining his trust and proving my loyalty in the Bandidos, William knew I was the only person in his organization that could pull this off. My ability to speak the language, plus my level of courage and ability to control my nerves under pressure made me the perfect man for the job.

So early the next morning, we boarded the plane in Bogota and departed for Barranquilla. Since this was a domestic flight, the passengers were mostly Colombians on their way to the sunny beaches on the Caribbean coast of Colombia.

Before we took off, the atmosphere in the cabin was stiflingly hot. There is no medium ground with some Columbians when it comes to personal odors, and the aroma of heavily applied perfume filtered through the cabin, along with some more odorous natural scents.

In 1980, flying on the airlines was drastically different from the experience of today, and smoking in the cabins was still permitted. Most of what I saw outside my window was viewed through a gossamer veil of thick smoke. Regardless, the vast panorama of the Colombian landscape passing beneath the wings was breathtaking. The predominant color of Columbia is green. Every shade of green. It undulated from horizon to horizon, thousands of feet below us in a verdant carpet that crept up to the snowcapped peaks jutting from the jungle. For a small-town boy from Texas, it was exhilarating.

Rivers and streams became shining silver ribbons of light that wound through the trees, and only occasionally would we catch sight of a paved road or village in the middle of the forest.

The Ernesto Cortissoz International Airport in Barranquilla was built in 1919, making it the first airport in South America. At that time, there were no jetways for disembarking passengers, so as soon as the cabin doors opened, we were greeted by a wave of tropical humidity unlike any I had felt before. Right away my clothes began to stick to my body as we descended the airstairs and crossed the tarmac into a terminal building filled with the ever-present, gun-toting soldiers to collect our bags before heading for the bus station.

Barranquilla is a city of two million people with the largest seaport on the northern coast of Columbia. Once one of the most modern cities in Columbia, a series of corrupt administrations had been responsible for a decline in the standard of living. Today, her national position has changed dramatically. The air is rank with diesel fumes and the streets are littered with trash. The atmosphere is permeated with a visceral feeling of danger, especially for gringos. I was fortunate to have Sonny with me, because without him, I probably wouldn't be telling this story.

The bus station was a madhouse surrounded by double-parked vehicles and filled with shouting people, squealing animals, and the inevitable presence of armed men. I spent a lot of time trying to figure out if they were army, paramilitary, mercenaries, or just private thugs hired to keep the peace as we worked our way through the labyrinth of ticket windows to the rows of waiting busses.

After a sweaty half-hour of searching, we finally found the bus for Santa Marta and El Rodadero Beach, and climbed aboard along with about sixty other passengers. As you've probably guessed by now, the bus wasn't air conditioned and we had to keep the windows down for our trip through the smog-filled city, but as soon as we left the city behind and began to travel along the coast road, the air became cooler and much easier to breathe.

With my light skin and blue eyes, I stood out like a sore thumb, making it obvious I was the only gringo on the bus. I was also probably the only person within a hundred miles that had as many tattoos as I did. I have spider web designs on both elbows, as well as many other large tattoos dispersed with smaller ones on both arms, and on the webs of my fingers. I tried to hide them with long sleeve shirts traveling through airports and in the cooler temperatures of Bogota, but the long sleeves were not an option in the heat and humidity in the coastal jungles, despite the close scrutiny I received in one of our frequent interactions with Columbian authorities.

Although the highways of Colombia provide a pleasant view of some of the most beautiful scenery I've ever seen, a peaceful bus journey is often interrupted by roadblocks manned by anyone from the military to a group of men with automatic weapons demanding payment to travel their section of the road. The bus driver would stop and these men would board the bus to walk up and down the aisles, intimidating passengers while the driver was negotiating with the leader for the cost to continue along that stretch of road. Once they reached an agreement and were paid, they would then lift the makeshift barricade and the bus would be allowed to proceed.

At other times, the bus would have to stop at an established outpost with a lift gate manned by the Colombian police. At these stops, the uniformed and heavily-armed troops would board the bus to search and interrogate whomever they pleased. Guess who got interrogated and searched! This is when my friend Sonny became my savior, and the special visa stamped on my passport by Arnulfo was used as an indicator that I was no ordinary gringo.

These were also the times when those Buck knives and Ray Ban sunglasses we bought in Panama became as valuable as gold. After the initial questioning and show of force was over, and the man in charge was wearing a brand new pair of shades and stuffing a twenty-dollar bill in his pocket, I was suddenly a respected visiting dignitary.

In addition to police, there are the Carabineros, soldiers of the official army of Columbia. On the outskirts of every city along the coast, these troops stop and inspect all traffic, releasing them only when they are satisfied that they aren't criminals or drug dealers. At every one of these stops, I was questioned at length and my papers were closely scrutinized by heavily-armed soldiers. After a bit of rapid-fire Spanish and posturing by the man in charge, Sonny's offer of some knives and shades had us on our way once again. If you're ever planning on traveling through Columbia on the jungle roads, best stock up on Buck knives and sunglasses.

We eventually arrived at the coastal tourist town of Rodadero Beach, a small tourist resort just over the mountain from Santa Marta, a major destination for foreign tourists as well as for members of the Colombian upper class. We were met at the bus station by two young cartel men named Miko and Lucho. They both appeared to be in their mid-twenties and were casually dressed in clothes that were several notches above what the other people in the station were wearing

Although Rodadero Beach catered to the affluent and wealthy, the residents were anything but, making it obvious that Miko and Lucho were from somewhere else. Miko was skinny and always laughing, while the more serious Lucho was muscular to the point that he reminded me of a young Mohamed Ali. Although they were not African American, their black heritage was apparent, as it was with so many people we came across in South America.

The two of them, along with Sonny, proved to be excellent companions, guides and protectors for me while I was in their company. I was treated more like a visiting family member than a hostage, and although it was obvious from their dress and mannerisms that they were both cartel members, I never felt uncomfortable around them.

After a short ride from the bus station, we arrived at a small apartment complex on the side of the main highway leading into town. With white stucco walls and a red tiled roof, the complex was surrounded by a gated flower-filled courtyard with a fountain in the middle. One had only to walk around the courtyard and inhale the aromas from the jungle to know that one was truly in the tropics.

The apartment had two air-conditioned bedrooms and a living room with large screened windows which were left open to catch the breeze blowing off the Caribbean. This was where Miko and Lucho would string their hammocks at night.

Our cook/housekeeper was Lupe, who was there from dawn to dusk to make meals and do all the laundry and other chores around the place. She spoke no English and was a delightful lady who always smiled and nodded her head as she spoke. She cooked mostly local dishes and was anxious to learn a few from Texas that I taught her to make.

We had a phone in the apartment, but I never made any calls. The only messages we received came through Sonny. The little black and white television only picked up local stations in Spanish and held little interest for me. Instead, I read books in English and received a day-old Miami Herald every morning to keep up with news back in the states.

Most days started with a breakfast of eggs, fried plantains, Lupe's homemade bread with jam, plus some strong Columbian coffee. Due to the fact that we were staying in a tourist town to avoid suspicion, the majority of our meals during the day were taken at small beach cafes and little cooking huts, where fresh fish, crab, calamari and lobster were always on the menu. From the munchies I acquired after smoking the local Santa Marta Gold marijuana, I was a frequent customer in all of these establishments.

The lazy days went by surprisingly fast, and my Colombian friends were always up for a party. I drank the local alcoholic beverage called Agua Diente, a clear liqueur that tasted like licorice and reminded me of absinthe or Pernod. Needless to say, the drink had a kick. We would drink it from the lid of the bottle in shots, then toss the few remaining drops into a corner for those who were not there to share, then pass the bottle. After several capfuls, I would begin to feel a whole new world around me. I have had lots of experiences with hallucinogens, and the feeling was pretty reminiscent of some trips I had taken in the past.

On day forty-six, I received a call from William with instructions to return to Bogota and meet him at the Hotel Tequendama. Sonny and I reluctantly bid our two protectors a fond farewell and used up our remaining sunglasses and Buck knives to make our way back along the soldier-encrusted roads to the airport in Barranquilla.

I missed the Caribbean breezes the moment I stepped out of the airport into the diesel-scented air of Bogota. With William, money was always plentiful. That night we went to a club in a fashionable neighborhood, where we smoked weed, enjoyed ninety-dollar bottles of Chivas Regal, and freebased cocaine.

The next day, William and I separated at the airport and I boarded the plane to Panama. The flight back to Panama City was interesting, to say the least. I took my seat in a Boeing 747 that was about half-filled with passengers, and everyone was in a good mood as we waited on the tarmac to take off.

As our scheduled take-off time passed, we all started to wonder what the hold-up was. Back then, most airliners usually took off on time, even in Columbia. After waiting for about thirty minutes, the captain announced that there was a mechanical problem and that the ground crew was investigating. Fortunately, the air conditioning was still on, and we were all quite comfortable.

Because Colombia is an international destination, there were a variety of nationalities on board, including a string quartet from a Viennese orchestra. After another thirty minutes of waiting, the flight attendants announced that they would be serving free champagne and first-class appetizers to the entire plane.

The mood in the plane began to improve, and after the second round of champagne, everyone began to forget about the delay. The string quartet retrieved their instruments from the overheads and began to play, and everyone had a great time enjoying live classical music, free champagne and appetizers. Two hours later, it was a happy group of passengers that took off for an uneventful flight to Panama.

I stayed at the Holiday Inn airport hotel in Panama City for three days so as not to arouse any suspicion by immediately taking a flight back to the States after spending time in Colombia. The delay was probably a good thing. I had to see a doctor at the airport for some antibiotics because it seemed I had picked up a "souvenir of Bogota". Thank God for modern medicine.

Back in Miami, I had to go through customs and immigration, which didn't really concern me because I wasn't carrying anything that would get me in trouble. After passing through both checkpoints, I was walking down a long hallway toward the exit when a metal door off to the side opened. A serious-looking man in a dark suit motioned me into a Customs office and told me that they had some questions for me.

Naturally, they were interested in what I had been up to in Central and South America. My cover story was always partying, gambling, chasing women and having a good time. I was on vacation and always wanted to see that part of the world. They asked how much money I had on me and I told them I probably had a few thousand. Their reply was, "We think more like a few hundred thousand."

I was thoroughly strip searched and my bags were turned inside out. Needless to say, nothing was found. After about forty-five minutes of wasting my time, they had to let me leave. My only thought as I was walking out of their office was that those guys needed to take some intimidation classes from the Colombians.

I spent the remainder of my time in Miami at an airport lounge, reliving some of the memories of my time in Colombia while I waited for my return flight to Corpus Christi. After catching a connecting flight in

Houston, I was definitely drunk by the time I arrived back in Corpus. I suppose the stress of my time in a third-world country, plus the intimidation attempts by the Customs agents in Miami had finally emerged, and I let it all go as I made my way back to Texas.

CHAPTER 17

It seemed like I had been gone for years when I arrived back in Corpus Christi. One of William's friends picked me up at the airport, and in the surreal transfer of emotions that accompanies a return from a vastly different culture, I resumed my laid-back lifestyle in Port Aransas.

Without me around, my dog had gone missing, but my girlfriend, Sheri, was still there waiting for me. She never really asked for any details of my adventures. I couldn't have told her much anyway. Drug dealers don't supply information to girlfriends because they inevitably become ex-girlfriends. She was smart enough to put two and two together, but was more interested in the gifts I brought back for her.

After a few days of much needed R and R, I resumed doing business with my friend at the shrimp packing plant and began selling shrimp on the side of the road again. Island life was in full swing with spring break and all the college kids in town, and all of us locals enjoyed the influx of beautiful young people and all the money they brought with them.

The primary source of employment for locals was all service oriented. We were the faces behind the bars, waiting tables, renting surfboards, and of course, selling them some high-grade weed. Mixed with the breeze of salt air and suntan lotion was the scent of money.

Living back in Port Aransas was a comfortable reprieve from the time I spent in Columbia. I was finally back in my own world of sand, sun and surf, and enjoyed just being lazy again without the need for protectors around me. Money and weed continued to flow from William on a regular basis to help keep the shrimp and weed business afloat, and Sheri and I were enjoying a carefree lifestyle on island time.

We continued our motorcycle journeys and participated in functions around town like the Bar Room Bicycle Race, an event sponsored by Lone Star Beer. The rules were simple. Contestants left from a specific bar and followed a predetermined course, stopping at various bars around town. At each stop, the racers were required to down a specified amount of beer before continuing on to the next bar, until the winner reached the last bar.

Of course, the diabolical nature of the event's rules prevented any type of record-breaking speed. Making it to the finish line was mainly an exercise in alcoholic endurance. In truth, most of the "racers" were more interested in taking their time and enjoying all the free beer. Either way, a great time was had by all in an event that basically celebrated DUI.

In addition to these kinds of events, there was the famous "Deep Sea Roundup", a major fishing tournament that had been a tradition on the island for decades. Fishing for tarpon and sailfish off the coast of Texas had been attracting millionaire fishermen and celebrities like President Franklin Roosevelt to Port Aransas since the 1930s. For three days, high speed, million-dollar, deep sea fishing boats raced to the fishing grounds out in the Gulf in hopes of snagging the winning sailfish and making it back to the dock before the four o'clock gun went off. To say there was a lot of money to be made during the time the tournament was in town is an understatement.

For the remainder of 1980 and the summer of 1981, the fun continued. So did my business of selling shrimp and weed in San Antonio. I was returning from one of those trips on the ferry heading to the island when I thought I saw Sheri on the ferry passing us going the other way toward the mainland. As soon as I walked through the door of our cottage, I saw that all her belongings were gone. The only thing she left behind was a note saying she didn't want to be with me anymore.

Another woman had walked out on me and my already low self-esteem plummeted. Of course, I would never let that show, and I jumped right back into the island life and the drug scene with both feet. I already had the best weed around, and every bartender in town knew me, so the drinks were usually free.

I started doing some shrimping out in the Gulf at night with some old friends on little bay boats. We would shrimp all night, unload in the morning, get paid, then drive to Corpus Christi in my van and score heroin. After we got loaded, we'd sleep all day and go back shrimping at night.

By then, I had started shooting heroin intravenously and was buying stolen narcotics, including morphine and hydromorphone. I knew I was in trouble. My drug use had become insane. The self-preservation side of my brain was screaming out to me, and I began a slow detox away from opiates. Thinking back on it, I was as close as I ever had been to going off the deep end.

Sometime after this, in the summer of 1981, I met Michelle, a beautiful girl with long blond hair, big green eyes and high cheekbones.

She had a little two-year-old girl named Amanda, and the two of them would eventually become important fixtures in my life. We hit it off right away and the three of us spent a lot of time together that summer.

Truth was, I desperately needed a real relationship after Sheri left me. I'm no good at being alone, and my codependency and low self-esteem leads me to cling to any woman who shows an interest. After taking a long hard look at my past track record, I decided to play it cool this time and avoided moving in with her to see where things led.

In the late fall of that year, William asked me to go back to South America for another big weed deal. This time my destination was San Jose in Costa Rica, where I spent a week waiting for further instructions from William. He gave me ten thousand dollars that I smuggled out of the country to live on and to pay my old acquaintance Arnulfo, the DAS agent in Bogota.

While I waited in San Jose, I visited their national museum, toured the breweries, and picked up a girl at a gentlemen's club called The Lone Star. She followed me back to the KLM Hotel and hung out with me for the next four days. I also took a bus to Puntarenas on the Pacific Coast. Back then, it was still a fishing village near the Gulf of Nicoya with long beautiful beaches known for strong surf. The tides are about fifteen feet each day, and the deep blue water of the Pacific makes it a perfect spot for deep sea fishing. I enjoyed myself so much there that I decided to check into the Hotel Colonial for the rest of my stay in Costa Rica. I still think about that little beach town and sometimes think of returning to see what it's like today.

After staying in Puntarenas for nine days, I finally received word from William and flew to Panama, where I checked into the Panama City Holiday Inn at the airport. A week later, William arrived and we moved to the Holiday Inn in the city, where he spent the next few days transferring money from his offshore accounts to his contacts in Colombia.

We did the usual partying, and William actually became a minor celebrity for his marathon marijuana smoking, cocaine use and drinking. After a few days of this debauchery, I was finally given the greenlight to continue my journey. The following day, I flew into El Dorado airport in Bogota.

Once again, I was met by Arnulfo, who walked me through customs and immigration and procured a ninety-day stamp on my Visa instead of the usual thirty-day one. And once again, there was no bag search when he flashed his government credentials and walked me through the diplomatic section of customs, and we sailed right out of the airport.

After taking a cab into the center of the city, I checked into the prestigious Hotel Taquendema and settled into another luxurious room upstairs. After the required pleasantries, I gave Arnulfo fifteen hundred dollars and he thanked me and left. That was the last time I ever saw him, and to this day I wonder what ever happened to him.

Later that day, an American named Willy showed up. He was another friend and associate of William's I had met previously when Sheri and I took a lot of money to Grand Cayman for William earlier that year. Willy and I made the tourist scene around Bogota, posing as tourists on a visit to Monserrate and eating at expensive restaurants.

We were finally instructed to meet a young man named Marco, the son of an influential man in the weed business. Marco informed me that his father had stockpiles of weed scattered around the jungle on the other side of the mountains near a little village they kept secret. My job was to go there, test the weed, and if acceptable, make the usual purchase arrangements before loading it onto one of William's shrimp boats for shipment to the States.

Together, we all took a cab to a small airport on the outskirts of Bogota and boarded a twin engine, pressurized, six-passenger aircraft that would fly us to the city of Villavicencio. Enroute to Villavicencio, we noticed a jet plane with the markings of the Colombian Air Force on the fuselage. The jet seemed to be following us, however our pilot kept trying to reassure us that it was nothing to be concerned about. After several tense minutes, the jet eventually peeled off and we went on our way without seeing it again.

When we landed in Villavicencio, we were met by another pilot and changed planes. If the military was trying to follow us, this plane change was designed to throw them off. The new plane was a single engine Piper with only four seats, and where the last flight was comfortable, air conditioned and pressurized, we were now flying in a coughing bare-bones aircraft at tree-top level across the plains of Colombia.

CHAPTER 18

Once in the air again, I soon learned that our destination was a little village called Mapiripam, located on the banks of the Guaviare River. The airport was nothing more than a grass strip. The men wore guns openly, and the only law enforcement was apparently provided by a few soldiers hanging around a cantina with their weapons slung over their shoulders. The place had no electricity, no plumbing, and apparently, no roads leading into or out of it. I had no idea where we were going or how long our business would take, but our pilot informed us that he would only wait until twilight because the so-called airport had no lighting.

Exchanging glances with Marco, we followed two Columbian villagers through the village to a dock down by the river. Needless to say, two gringos in a remote Colombian village drew a lot of stares from the locals. Tied to the dock was a long canoe called a cayuca by the locals. A cayuca is a canoe carved from a single tree trunk about three feet wide and fifteen feet long, and the power was provided by a thirty-five horsepower Yamaha outboard engine mounted on the rear transom.

Two men armed with rifles were waiting for us in the boat, so Willy and I climbed aboard with Marco, and together we all headed upriver to a secret location where the weed was supposedly stashed. The river was about two hundred yards wide with a swift current, making our trip upriver slow going even with the outboard running full tilt.

The river was a geographical dividing line in the landscape. Grassy plains stretched off to infinity on one side, providing an unlimited view. On the other side, there's an impenetrable jungle crowding the banks. I remember thinking that, if the canoe were to capsize or sink for some reason, no one would ever know what happened to me.

As we were heading upstream against the sound of the straining engine, I heard a sharp click behind me. The first thought in my mind was that someone behind me was chambering a round in his rifle, and that Willy and I were about to be shot. I slowly glanced over my shoulder and saw one of the men clicking a lighter in an attempt to light his cigarette in the wind. Sometimes, traveling to a secret jungle drug hideout up a Columbian river with two armed strangers, your mind can play tricks on you.

After an hour of chugging up the river, they nosed our boat into a niche in the bank that I didn't even see at first. The boat was tied off to a tree and we set off on a muddy trail through the thick jungle. I could almost feel the jungle creatures watching us as we trudged through the undergrowth, until suddenly, we were in a clearing. Standing right in front of us was an A-frame structure packed with bales of marijuana.

After glancing back at our smiling guides, Willy and I began cutting into one of the bales at the top of the stack to test for smell, color and seed content. I then took out a pack of Zig Zag papers and rolled a few joints for Willy and I to smoke. Strangely, the Colombians did not smoke their own product and only watched as we lit our joints. I will never forget getting high in the middle of a Colombian jungle while sitting on top of ten thousand pounds of marijuana.

After giving Marco our stamp of approval, we made our way back to the boat and began our return trip downstream to Mapiripam. Even with the swift current now in our favor, we didn't make it back to the village until after sunset, where we were informed that the pilot had returned to Villavicencio after leaving word that he would pick us up the next morning.

That night, we smoked weed and drank warm beer, along with capfuls of potent aguardiente in a little cantina with a generator. I will always remember a sign on the wall that said in Spanish: "Si toma para olvidar, pague antes de olvide." Translated, it means: "If you drink to forget, pay before you forget." Years later, I had this sign printed and displayed in a bar that I ran for seven years.

We all got sickeningly wasted that night before staggering in the dark to a dormitorio, a sort of hotel where we crashed on hard wooden bunks draped with mosquito netting for the price of a few dollars. Thankfully, I was so wasted that sleeping on the hard bunk didn't faze me. However, when I woke up, I was sore as hell all over.

A few hours after breakfast, the same little Piper returned to take us back to Villavicencio. However, as usual, things are never as simple as they appear to be in Colombia. The plane had only four seats, but we were told we would have to take another Columbian back with us. With five on board, the scenery scrolled by our windows slowly as we attempted to take off, and after what I figured to be an extra two hundred yards, we lifted off into the sky. I thank God we were on the flat side of the river, because if there had been trees at the end of the runway as is so often the case, our crash would have become part of local lore.

When we arrived at the airport in Villavicencio, we were met by Colombian officials who wanted to know why the little plane with gringos on board was taking off and returning the next day to their airport. I was having a hard time translating the rapid-fire Spanish, but in the end, the universal language of American cash was the deciding factor and the inspectors all left smiling.

Our twin engine plane was not available to fly us back over the mountains to Bogota, so we found a taxi driver that agreed to drive us. It was a long drive but it provided me with the opportunity to take a lot of pictures that I still have to this day. Along the way, we stopped in a little mountain village to enjoy a lunch of black beans, rice and Columbian beer. In Columbia, you never knew what you would get when it came to public restrooms, and at this stop we were greeted with holes in the floor with no running water or toilet paper.

After crossing the mountains, our descent took us into the worst part of Bogota. Stark poverty was the order of the day, and the living conditions were deplorable. The taxi driver intentionally ran stop signs and traffic lights for fear of stopping in one place too long. We finally reached the Hotel Tequendama in the more affluent part of the city, and one night of rest was all I got. The next day, I said goodbye to Willy at the airport and he returned to the States. A few hours later, I boarded a flight to Barranquilla.

Back in the crazy world of Barranquilla, my old friends Miko and Lucho met me at the airport and I checked into a fairly nice hotel in town. That night, I met with another Colombian named Chapa, who had made arrangements for me to travel up the coast to the small coastal village of Manaure, in the La Guajira Peninsula. However, to get there required some logistical planning that only the Columbians could have arranged.

We took the bus to my old stomping grounds in the beach city of Rodadero, where I stayed in a private family home. The home was built in a square with all the rooms situated around a pool in a central courtyard. For anyone who has ever traveled in Mexico or Central and South America, this layout would be very familiar. After a brief and relaxing stay, we headed off through the jungle in a Jeep Cherokee.

It was no surprise when we arrived in yet another Wild West town called Riohacha. The surprise was that the town had electricity, plumbing, and even a few traffic lights. The men still openly wore side arms, and once again, soldiers carrying automatic weapons seemed to be the only law enforcement. Fortunately for me, I was under Chapa's protection, so no one hassled me.

I spent most of the day there inspecting bales of marijuana in the various stash houses. At one house, my chaperone didn't have the key for one of the rooms and was freaking out and yelling at the other men who were frightened of him. I told him to calm down and put a well-placed kick next to the doorknob. The door frame splintered and the door flew open. The surprised man looked at me with a big smile and put his arm around my shoulders, and we all had a big laugh.

Once again, I had to show these guys that I wasn't afraid and couldn't be pushed around or be trifled with. The macho image is a predominant trait in Central and South American countries, where kindness is often mistaken for weakness in some circles.

After a day of inspecting, smoking and marking bales, we rested for the night before setting off the next day for the last leg of our trip to Manaure.

As I have described at length before, the roads in Colombia are challenging at best. The farther north we went, the worse the roads became. Entire sections of roads had been washed away during the rainy season, and we still had to face the occasional hasty roadblock manned by soldiers looking to make a quick buck. Although I was still under Chapa's protection, the occasional twenty-dollar bill or Buck knife was always welcomed.

We eventually came to a small house, where we exchanged the Jeep Cherokee for a Toyota Land Cruiser, the acknowledged workhorse of Colombian drug smugglers. With the required four-wheel drive, high road clearance and diesel engine, it was the perfect machine for traveling through the jungle.

We drove on a rutted road for miles, catching glimpses of men posted in the trees with rifles or machine guns before finally arriving at a little shack filled with bales of marijuana. After a quick smoke, we turned around and headed back to the waiting Cherokee.

I slept well that night in Riohacha and awakened the next morning to the aroma of strong Colombian coffee. The coffee in Columbia was enough to keep me awake all day. Colombian coffee that we buy in the U.S. isn't even close to the real deal. Columbian coffee in Columbia, known as Tinto among the natives, is every coffee drinker's dream. In that respect, it's kind of like their marijuana. Nothing else quite compares.

After breakfast, we set out on our final leg to the quiet fishing village of Manaure on the western Caribbean coast of the Quajire Peninsula. We arrived in the early afternoon and met with some Colombians who had a small, eighteen-foot-long fiberglass fishing boat powered by an outboard engine.

Equipped with marine band radios, they were currently in touch with the steel hull shrimp boat that would be transporting the marijuana I had just purchased back to the States. The name of the boat was the Disco Lady. Coming out of Louisiana, she was eighty-five feet long with a twenty-five-foot beam and was completely set up for deep-sea offshore trawling. The space below decks was capable of holding thousands of pounds of ice and shrimp. She was also capable of holding thirty-five thousand pounds of high-grade marijuana.

The Colombians quickly informed us that the boat was only a few miles offshore and had been sailing up and down the coast following the same coordinates, waiting to hear from me. As soon as I contacted them, they turned and headed for our rendezvous point along the line they had been traveling.

Miko and I quickly hopped into the small boat and we shoved off from the beach into the clear turquoise waters of the Caribbean Sea. Fortunately, the sea wasn't too rough and the weather was clear. Nevertheless, riding in a small boat in the open ocean is almost never a smooth ride. After two hours of waves splashing over the bow, we saw a black dot on the horizon. As it turned out, the Disco Lady had already passed the rendezvous point and we were coming up on her stern.

For the next couple of hours, we chased her until we either finally showed up on her radar or someone happened to glance off the stern and saw us. She slowed and we came up on her leeward side where Miko and I jumped aboard. Once on deck, I was reunited with my friend Jughead, a man from Aransas Pass that I had known for many years, plus Jerry, my old Bandido brother. Like me, Jerry had also retired in good standing from the club, and I had suggested to William that he would make a good member of our crew because he had proven his loyalty on numerous occasions when we rode together.

I was also thrilled to be able to speak English again with old friends. The burden of having to constantly translate everything from Spanish to English in my mind had become a bit of a chore, to say the least. We continued to sail along at a leisurely pace until we reached a spot off the coast of Riohacha. This was the rendezvous point where the marijuana would be loaded and I could feel the excitement building. My cut for the load was ten dollars a pound, meaning I was looking at a three-hundred-and-fifty-thousand-dollar payday … my swan song in the smuggling industry and the key to my future.

We timed our arrival at the rendezvous point just after dark and dropped anchor a mile or so off the coast. After some coordination with the ground crew, we began to see a number of small boats approaching in the Caribbean darkness. Together, we all began loading the marijuana at a fast and furious pace. Even though our contacts had paid off or frightened off any rival smugglers, we still had to be cautious of the Colombian Navy, who routinely patrolled these waters.

Working through the night, we filled the holds with bale after bale, hiding it everywhere we could, including under the flooring of the wheelhouse and cabins, finally finishing up just before dawn. With no time to waste, I told my old friends on the boat that I would see them when they got to the States and wished them a bon voyage and good luck before returning to the beach.

Other than the ubiquitous roadblocks, the trip back down the coast to Santa Marta and Rododero Beach was uneventful. I spent the next few days at a hotel in Rododero, relaxing on the beach and smoking weed. Eventually, I took the bus back to Barranquilla and caught a flight back to Bogota. My flight to Miami left in the early afternoon, so I napped in the first-class lounge while waiting. There had been no contact with anyone in the States as to the disposition of the Disco Lady. All I could do now was cross my fingers and wait.

CHAPTER 19

Back in Miami, I passed through Customs and Immigration quickly, but I was ready for anything after the ordeal I went through before. I held my breath walking past the door I had been taken through for a strip search the last time, but sailed right past and out into the cool fall air of Florida.

I was overjoyed to be back in my own country once again. In my mind, I was already counting my share of the money and spending it on all kinds of goodies. While I was still at the Miami airport, I called William to let him know I was back in the country. As soon as I stepped off the plane in Corpus Christi, Michelle was waiting for me.

As we headed over the Corpus Christi Harbor Bridge to Aransas Pass, she looked across at me and smiled. She was pregnant. I was still a little drunk from the number of drinks I had consumed on the flight, so the news didn't register right away. I remember looking out the window at the ships in the harbor below when she dropped the bombshell. I was the father.

After hearing that she was three months along, I sobered up a little and did the math. Sure enough, it fit the time we had been together. Even though I had already been married twice, neither of my wives had gotten pregnant. In fact, I had become convinced that I was incapable of fathering a child. I asked again if she was absolutely sure. She was adamant. I was the daddy.

Naturally I let her know I would take care of her and the baby. Truth be told, I had always wanted to be a father with a wife and children to take care of. I had always wanted to be like my father, a man who had always been a great provider for his family.

It goes without saying that this was a major turning point in my life. I had just been involved in a major smuggling run and stood to make a third of a million dollars in cash, and now I had the added responsibility of caring for a wife, a little stepdaughter, plus a child on the way.

It suddenly felt as if I was on a precipice of sorts. My life had been full of insecurities … feeling "less than others", and I had compensated for this with criminal and violent behavior that had landed me in prison. I felt as though I hadn't had a single successful relationship in my entire life. I owned nothing. No land, no home, no furniture, no savings … no steady income at all other than what I made dealing drugs. With the effects from the alcohol wearing off, the thought hit me like a sledge hammer. Obviously, I was going to have to make some changes. Question was; could I do it?

My head was still swimming when Michelle dropped me off at William's house, where I learned that the boat would be landing somewhere near Morgan City, Louisiana in a few days. Until then, it was our duty as international drug smugglers to smoke weed, snort cocaine, and drink as much booze as we could. I had missed the company of my good friends while I was gone, and that night we all got quite wasted.

The next day, I made it over to Michelle's apartment in nearby Ingleside. I remember that it was almost Christmas. She had a tree with decorations, and there were presents for me and Amanda under the tree.

Thankfully, William had given me some more cash for my work in Colombia, so I was able to buy them both a lot of presents. I spent Christmas with them that year and we enjoyed our time together. In fact, those are some of the best memories of my life.

A few days after Christmas, duty called and I was on my way to Baton Rouge, Louisiana with William and a guy named Mike, another friend from high school days. I discovered over time that my friends from high school were the most loyal, even the one who became a cop. Those who are still alive remain my friends today, and I would trust them with my life.

In Baton Rouge, we checked into a motel and waited while William made arrangements with his Louisiana connections to unload the boat. Any time not spent doing important smuggling work is always spent getting high and hanging out in bars wherever we went, and this was no exception. On one particular afternoon, Mike and I got really wasted in his room smoking some good weed, then spent the rest of the day drinking in a bar, trying to meet women.

Later that evening, William returned and told us he had made arrangements to unload the boat at a shrimp dock in Morgan City, and we needed to be up early to go there. Strangely, William had been unable to make contact with the Disco Lady for several days, a fact we casually attributed to radio problems or weather.

The next morning, we headed down south to the house of the man who owned the dock where we would be offloading the boat. William had brought along a briefcase full of money to make payoffs to the workers at the dock, and he had entrusted it to Mike. When he asked

Mike to get it from the car, Mike returned empty-handed. As it turned out, he had stashed the briefcase under the bed at the motel and was so hungover from the night before that he had left it there.

What a dilemma for Mike. We couldn't exactly go back and ask the manager if anyone had found a briefcase with several thousand dollars in cash in the room. Two scenarios popped into our minds. Either the hotel maids were celebrating, or the briefcase had already been turned in to the authorities. Either of these scenarios we held a large degree of risk if we went back to look for it. If the authorities had it, questions about why we were carrying around so much money would have cast suspicion on us and endangered the entire operation.

Long story short, William had to take the loss and Mike probably did a lot of free work for him after that. Fortunately, William always carried other briefcases no one else knew about when he was involved in a smuggling operation of this magnitude. With his experience, he never knew who we might have to pay off at the last minute.

We spent the rest of that day with the dock owner, watching TV and smoking weed, which is pretty much what we did most of the time anyway. Late that afternoon, William walked in and gave us the news. He had just been contacted by the wife of one of the men on the boat. She informed him that the boat had been busted by the Coast Guard sailing through the Yucatan Pass between Mexico and Cuba.

What a bummer! I had just lost three hundred and fifty thousand dollars, and now I had to worry about someone on board the boat giving me up to the DEA in return for a lenient sentence. We immediately loaded up and began our trip back to Texas, wondering what to do next while our minds were wracked with fear and paranoia.

I was also concerned about my old Bandido brother, Jerry, who had a wife and kid in Corpus Christi. I knew he would never give me or William up under interrogation. I was more worried about Jughead, who was an alcoholic and the captain, as well as someone I hadn't known as long as the others. All I knew was that he had gained William's trust, so I was forced to rely on that. I also didn't know if William was making plans to see to their needs, both financially and legally through a third party, usually an attorney in these cases. Making sure they knew they hadn't been abandoned went a long way toward making sure they kept their mouths shut.

When we arrived back home, I made the decision then and there that I was going to get as far away from Aransas Pass as possible and give up the smuggling life for good. I had a baby on the way and had made a commitment to Michelle that I would be there for her, Amanda and my baby. Over time, I had acquired a strong sense of loyalty, whether it be to an outlaw motorcycle club, a criminal smuggling enterprise, or to a woman I cared about and her children. I was determined not to let them down.

CHAPTER 20

Armed with a new sense of loyalty to my new way of life, I began making plans to go somewhere else to start anew. I drove to Corpus Christi and sold my Rolex and gold Thai chain for eight thousand dollars to a jeweler that Michelle knew. As soon as I got back, we loaded up my van and took off for the home of some friends in Farmington, New Mexico.

It was now late December of 1981, and the farther north we traveled, the colder it got and the worse the road conditions became. I had a big cargo van with two front seats and an open back section with no side windows or insulation. We had the dashboard heater going full blast, but we were still cold most of the time.

Once we reached El Paso, I stopped and bought a little Coleman heater in hopes of keeping the rear section of the van reasonably warm. In my haste, I hadn't thought to talk to William or get any more cash, so for the first time in a long time, I was forced to conserve money. We ate sandwiches picnic style most of the trip and slept in the van at night in roadside parks.

By now we were entering the snow country of New Mexico and I had to leave the engine running and the Coleman heater running all the time. I would wake myself up every couple of hours to roll the windows down and let in some fresh air. To this day I still thank God we all didn't die from carbon monoxide poisoning.

I was so proud of Amanda. She was only two-and-a-half years old, but she was a good little trooper through it all. When we stopped in Albuquerque and I got out to pump gas, I noticed that ice had formed icicle spinners on all my hubcaps. I had come a long way from the hot, steamy jungles of Columbia.

We finally made it to the trailer home of Michelle's friends in Farmington, just south of the Colorado border. These were the waning days of the hippie craze, and like most young people back then, they had no problem welcoming travelers into their home and giving us a room where we made a pallet on the floor.

The following day, I gave her husband a ride to work at a refinery and applied for a job, but none was available. I continued giving him rides to work the next few days and poked my nose into the personnel office to see if any new jobs had been posted, but when it came to jobs with decent pay, the employment well in Farmington was dry.

All the time our money was running out and I was burning a lot of gas taking him to work and picking him up each day. I talked with Michelle and we decided that we needed to do something else while we still had some money left. She called her father in Oklahoma City and begged him to let us stay with him until we could get on our feet again. After some debate, he finally agreed and we set off for Oklahoma City.

Our poverty-laced journey reminded me of the families heading west with all their belongings in "The Grapes of Wrath", except we were headed east, and our dust bowl was a snowstorm. We spent the first night on the road under the brilliant lights of a truck stop on I-40 in Amarillo. With the snow piling up on the interstate and the temperature dropping, Michelle, Amanda and I bundled up in our sleeping bags and quilts and managed to make it through the night in the warmth from the Coleman heater.

While we waited for the snowplows to clear the highway, we freshened up in the restrooms and ate breakfast in the truck stop cafe before setting off again. We arrived in Yukon, a suburb of Oklahoma City, later that day and drove to the home of Michelle's father. This was my first introduction to Bernie Drake. Bernie was a former marine in his fifties and had a beautiful brick home on a cul-de-sac in one of the nicer neighborhoods of Yukon. He had been divorced from Michelle's mother for quite some time and was happily married to a woman who was at least twenty-five years younger.

Bernie was an insurance agent who had done well for himself over the years. He was a man that knew how to make money, save money, and make his money work for him, and he had a penchant for long-winded, interesting stories. I didn't learn until many years later that he was also a recovering alcoholic. After assuring him that I intended to take care of Michelle, Amanda, and the baby on the way, he allowed us to stay in one of the bedrooms until we were able to get a place of our own.

As it turned out, Michelle had two younger brothers named Michael and Mark. Michael, it turned out, was an alcoholic and avid weed smoker, just like me. Naturally, one of the first things I noticed when we arrived was a tall marijuana plant next to the fence in the back yard. Even in my most desperate hours, it seemed that marijuana always found me.

The fence was about six feet tall and Michael had been trimming the top off the plant before it began poking up over the top of the fence. As a result, he had grown a beautiful sinsemilla plant of high-grade marijuana about six feet tall and eight feet wide.

The single plant actually looked like a hedge, and I was surprised to learn that Mr. Ex-Marine Bernie was aware of it. His rationale for permitting it was that he wanted his boys to grow their own weed so they wouldn't become involved in the dark business of drug dealers in the Oklahoma City area. Smart man. Too bad more fathers aren't that intelligent nowadays.

During those first few days at Bernie's, I managed to reach William by phone. I learned that the boat and load had indeed been confiscated and that the crew was in jail in Florida. As I had guessed, William figured out a way to help with bail and lawyers without anyone knowing that he was the one financing the legal team. Eventually, the crew was given probation and the government kept the boat and the weed.

Despite long hours of harassment by detectives and DEA agents, no one rolled over on me or William. They kept their mouths shut, and William's money and loyalty to his crew eventually bought them out of a very bad situation.

I informed William that I was out of the smuggling business and was going to start a new life. He wished us all well and said we should always keep in touch. I was never paid for my last trip to Colombia. Looking back on it, Willian had taken a terrific loss, not to mention all the money that went to the legal defense of the crew.

In the end, I guess it was worth it. At least I was in the clear as far as the authorities were concerned. I made contact with Jerry later and we both agreed our smuggling days were over for good. We pledged to always keep in touch, and I thanked him for his continued loyalty to me and our brotherhood.

Now ensconced in domestic bliss, Michelle and I settled in with Bernie and his wife, Vickie, for the next few weeks. I spent my days looking for some kind of work and eventually met a man named Shorty Long, who hired me to install microwave antennas in rural areas to pick up The Movie Channel.

My territory covered an area within a hundred-mile radius of Oklahoma City, so I spent my days driving the back roads while smoking Yukon Gold, the term we had given the weed from the backyard plant. This was ideal for me because I was able to work on my own, stay high all day, and no one bothered me. After a couple of months, I was able to rent a modest little red brick house with one bath and a one car garage. This was our first home as a new family and I was thrilled to be able to step into the role of being a good husband and provider, something I'd never done before.

By late winter of 1982, Michelle was seven months into her pregnancy and I was beginning to feel like she was "the one". I was also developing a relationship with Amanda, which also added to our happiness as a family. I had a job, we were able to pay our bills, and I had shown Bernie that I was a man of my word. Best of all, it felt like I had earned his respect.

I helped Michael and his brother Mark with the final harvest of the giant Yukon Gold plant, and we all had plenty of free weed for our smoking pleasure. I had not ridden a motorcycle in a long time, and although I missed the freedom of riding on the open road, I had replaced it with an inner satisfaction of perhaps finding the elusive American dream. I had always wanted to feel like I was important to others and never really knew how to go about doing it because of my lack of an inner compass and persistent feelings of low self-esteem.

Life became more and more centered around family. I spent more time at home and cut the grass on the weekends while Michelle kept the house clean. We even had friends over for barbecues and to watch sports on TV. What surprised me the most was how easy it had been to transition from being an international drug smuggler to a typical family man.

On May 11, 1983, Michelle began having labor pains and my beautiful daughter, Ashley Aline Spells, came squealing into this world. I had never expected to become a father, and at age 36, I finally was one. I fell in love with that little baby the moment I laid eyes on her. She was perfect in every way. I felt a sense of pride that I had never felt before, but above all, I knew that now someone would always love me. She was my little Pootsome-Tootsome girl, and today her nickname is Poots.

I remember taking my family to the Oklahoma State Fair and pushing Ashley proudly along in a stroller. I was so proud of my family and showed them off to everyone. We would go to the big city park on weekends and spend the entire afternoon having a picnic. We went to tractor pulls with Mark and Michael and spent time with Grandpa Bernie and Granny Vic every opportunity we had. My parents even came up for a visit in the fall. My old Bandido and smuggling past was finally behind me, and for a time, I was living the life I should have been living all along.

CHAPTER 21

In January of 1983, I heard from a friend in Aransas Pass that a company in Corpus Christi was running the same type of microwave antenna installations I was doing for a company called Vue. I called them and told them of my work experience in Oklahoma and was immediately offered a job making more money. Michelle and I talked it over and decided it would be a good move, so we rented a U-Haul truck and packed up to leave for South Texas.

Mark, myself and Ashley were in the rental truck, while Michael, Michelle and Amanda were following in my Ford van. The plan was to drive in a caravan the 700 plus miles to Ingleside, Texas and rent a house there. Somewhere out of Oklahoma City, Michael got separated from us and we had no way of knowing what had happened to them. Mark was driving and I was holding Ashley on the passenger side when we pulled over to wait for them. There was a small glass aquarium on the floorboard. Due to the stress of leaving my first real home, and out of my frustration of not knowing where the other vehicle was, I kicked the aquarium out on the side of the road, picked it up and smashed it into hundreds of pieces.

I suppose my explosive temper had been nurtured during my time in the Bandidos, when a quick angry reaction to a bad situation could usually settle things right then and there without ever having to fight, and this was the first time Mark had seen my other side. When I climbed back into the truck, Mark just looked away and didn't say a word to me for the next hundred miles.

We arrived in Ingleside later that day and Michael and Michelle showed up an hour later. The explanation was that they had to pull over to go to the bathroom and couldn't find us despite the fact that we had pulled over to wait.

We were lucky enough to find a rental house on a back road that ran parallel to the Intracoastal Waterway between Aransas Pass and Ingleside. We were back in South Texas, with the humid, salt-air breeze blowing off the same water I had worked on many times in the past.

I soon began working for the new company in Corpus Christi and made contact with William and a few other friends soon after my return. The guys on the boat had all been put on probation and were out of the smuggling business as well. My old Bandido brother Jerry was back in Corpus with his family and I visited him occasionally. He told me about the Coast Guard busting the boat coming through the Yucatan Pass and all they had to go through afterward. I am eternally grateful to those guys for keeping their mouths shut and not giving me up to the DEA. William never got out of the business, but I never helped him again. I was still able to score high-grade weed for my own use and to sell to friends as well.

After working for my new employers for a while, I began to notice a lack of accountability over inventory control, so one day I decided to pick up a couple of extra antennas along with all the necessary installation material to do a little illegal side work on my own. After all, a leopard doesn't change its spots so easily.

A typical install would usually cost around two hundred dollars. After sizing up one of my customers, I told him I could do his install off the books for a hundred dollars cash with no future monthly charges. He took me up on my offer and my latest criminal enterprise was off to the races.

I began stealing supplies on a regular basis and did at least one illegal install every other day. Some of my first customers would call me and give me the names of others who wanted to buy antennas, and after a while, I was making enough money for us to rent a nicer house from William's wife. As it turned out, William had been arrested for income tax evasion and was in federal prison in Bastrop, Texas, and she needed the money.

We moved into the house in April of 1983, just in time for Michelle to inform me that she was pregnant again. I was going to be a father once more. I had considered myself to be a loving dad with Amanda and Ashley, and was actually thrilled to know we were going to have another baby.

I continued to work for the same company in Corpus, doing legal as well as illegal installations of microwave antennas. I went to work five days a week and worked hard to pay the bills, but I was never able to save any money. Michelle was a hair stylist and had been cutting hair for quite a few years, so she was able to earn money on the side, but again it still seemed like we never had enough.

I still smoked weed on a daily basis and she smoked with me during both of her pregnancies. I had some friends who were heroin users and the pull was strong. Occasionally, I would get loaded with them, but more and more I was moving away from the world of hard drugs.

One day a friend of mine came by with some Guinea hens and a duck. He had no place to keep them and asked if I was willing to let them live on our place. I agreed. However, we soon learned the duck was a female and she expressed her gratitude with the gift of one egg each morning in the corner of the carport. I had never eaten duck eggs and was surprised to discover that they are delicious. A bit larger than chicken eggs with a much larger and tastier yolk. We would collect them for a few days and I would make these huge omelets for Sunday breakfasts.

We also discovered that Guinea hens are the perfect watchdogs. Their incessant squawking and gobbling would begin as soon as any strange person or animal set foot on our property. I also decided to do some farming that early spring. I borrowed a garden tractor from a friend and plowed some rows beside the house and planted tomatoes, carrots, radishes, bell peppers, cantaloupes, green beans. It seemed that life had once again settled into the rhythm of a carefree existence with my family, and I was determined to keep it that way.

Despite my steady job installing microwave antennas, both legally and illegally, we still struggled with finances. Michelle was still cutting hair to help out and we always had food on the table, but each week was a struggle to keep our heads above water. Early on in her pregnancy, we made the decision to have a home birth to save money because we couldn't afford all the hospital and medical bills.

The summer months passed into fall and the weather became a lot more comfortable. The nights were cooler and the days were not as oppressively hot as they had been all summer. Mark had come down from Oklahoma and was now staying with us since Michelle's due date was drawing near. He quickly found a job as a welder in a shipyard in Aransas Pass, and we all continued to smoke a lot of weed together while we waited for Michelle to give birth.

On October 14th of 1983, Michelle began having contractions in the afternoon and we called the midwife. She had left town and was in Dallas on business, so naturally we began to freak out. She insisted that everything would be fine if we listened to her and took things as they came. Luckily, Michelle also had some friends waiting in the wings to help us out as well.

The hours progressed and Mark was keeping Ashley occupied in the living room until she went to bed. We went outside to smoke a joint or two to calm my nerves, and at 3:28 in the morning, the strongest and most intense contraction began and Michelle pushed. Out came the head of this beautiful baby. Michelle continued to push, and within seconds, Allyson Arden Spells was in my hands. I remember looking up at the stars that night and thanking God for helping us to deliver a baby in our own home without any medical assistance.

Life continued on the same track that winter of 1983. For Christmas that year, we decided to travel back to Oklahoma City to spend the holidays with Bernie and Granny Vic. They had never met their newest granddaughter and were thrilled to have us for a few days. We had a wonderful Christmas with them, eating sumptuous Christmas meals and watching football games with Bernie, Mark and Michael.

While we were there, Michelle and I decided to get married. After obtaining all of the obligatory licenses and paperwork, we went to the home of a justice of the peace in Oklahoma City and he performed the ceremony in his living room. I had now been married three times in fifteen years.

We returned to South Texas and the new year had rolled around. By the spring of 1984, we were still in the same house where Allyson was born, and I was still doing legal and illegal installations of microwave antennas. Michelle and I were still getting high on weed daily, and occasionally even did some heroin and cocaine with some people I knew. In that respect, life really hadn't changed all that much for us. But once again, fate would intervene to bring a new dimension to my life.

CHAPTER 22

In April of 1984, I saw an ad in the Aransas Pass newspaper announcing open auditions for extras to work in a major motion picture to be filmed fifteen miles up the coast in Rockport, Texas. The town sits wedged between Aransas and Copano Bay and is home to a small bay shrimp boat fleet.

I decided to make the trip up to Fulton where the auditions were being held to see what was going on for myself. Apparently, I wasn't the only one. About one hundred and fifty curious men, women and children had also made the pilgrimage to catch a glimpse of the Hollywood elite.

We all gathered in the main hall of an event center there and were introduced to some of the production crew. They took the time to explain the mechanics of making a film, telling us about how one twenty-five-minute scene on screen could take days to film. The production man told us that, to get the best idea of what happens on a film, watch a movie with the sound off. Every time the scene changes on the screen, imagine that everything has to stop, be arranged or rearranged, then started over from the exact spot where the action stopped.

He went on to explain that there may be days when we would show up and not be used at all, but that we would get paid fifty dollars a day, regardless. We would also get breakfast, lunch and dinner if the shoot went into the evening. The production crew also provided snacks, drinks, and coffee at all times.

After this brief introduction, he asked how many of us were still interested. At least half of the attendees decided that this was not what they were willing to give up their day jobs for. The rest were probably like me, either not making a lot of money anyway, or just wanted to be a part of the magic.

Those of us remaining were separated into groups to meet with casting directors. We were given script lines and told we had a few minutes to memorize and practice them before being called by the directors. I was given a few lines of a fisherman talking to another fisherman, which made no sense to me taken out of context. At this point, none of us knew what the film was about. I practiced in the bathroom mirror for a few minutes before being called to the director's office, where he would read a line that I was supposed to respond to with the lines I had memorized.

After I was done, I was told to have a seat out in the main auditorium until they called me. I waited for about fifteen minutes and the director came out and told me that they were going to use me as an extra. They wanted me to return at 5 AM in three days to a small motel in Fulton, where the production company had rented all the rooms for a headquarters.

I soon learned the film was about the conflict between Texas Gulf Coast shrimpers and the Vietnamese fishermen who had immigrated to the town of Seadrift, Texas after the fall of Saigon in 1975. Seadrift is about thirty miles farther up the coast from the Rockport/Fulton area. After the Vietnamese arrived and began shrimping the long-held fishing grounds of the locals, violence erupted between the two factions, resulting in some deaths. Apparently, the Ku Klux Klan was also involved in many of the altercations at the time.

We also learned that the film was based on a story in Esquire magazine by author Ross Malloy, and was to feature some new faces in Hollywood. The faces belonged to Ed Harris, and his real-life wife, Amy Madigan, who was also starring in the film. The name of the movie was Alamo Bay.

I called my boss in Corpus and explained that I was going to take some time off and he was cool with that. I showed up at the scheduled time and met several other people who had been chosen for work as extras. I suppose they must have had a separate audition call for the Vietnamese extras, as I had not seen any at the auditions. The parking lot was crowded with both ethnic groups.

Funny how life imitates art. All the Vietnamese hung together and all the Anglos were hanging with their own crowd. This distinction held true for the duration of filming. There was never any open animosity, but the rift was palpable. I'm sure that, considering the close-knit nature of the Vietnamese culture, some of their kin were probably involved in what happened.

I became engrossed in the process of film making. I loved watching the actors prepare for their scenes and how they played them out before the camera. I was amazed at the intensity and concentration of the director. The movie was directed by Louis Malle, an accomplished French filmmaker of such movies as Pretty Baby and Atlantic City.

I found myself caught up in the machinations of a project involving lots of different people. I had never before been involved with a project that had union sanctions and union workers. For instance, a painter could not do any work that an electrician was supposed to do, and there were shop stewards on location to make sure none of the union rules were broken. The Teamsters did the driving. Painters painted, carpenters built, electricians wired, and guys called "grips" did most of the labor.

Since I wasn't available for filming every day, I would have to either check the schedule for the next day's shoot, or wait by the phone for one of the production assistants to call me and tell me where to show up. There were days that I would hang around all day and never be used in a shot, but I was still paid fifty dollars just for showing up.

One day, a production assistant approached me to say they had decided they wanted me to do a line in the movie. The setup for the scene was two bay shrimp boats bumping into each other. I was to be the captain of the boat that had just sideswiped a Vietnamese trawler. My line was to yell from the wheelhouse door, "Hey, Gook! Learn to drive!"

They had to do several takes to get the shot lined up just right, and I had to say the line over each time. The good news was that instead of being paid fifty dollars that day, I earned three hundred and fifty. That single line made me eligible to join the Screen Actors Guild, however at the time, I didn't have thousands of dollars to pay the union fee. If I had, I would have been eligible for any other movies filmed in Texas from then on. I also would have had an agent to help me find roles and keep my name in the hat for future projects. Looking back, I wish I would have taken more initiative and made that happen.

During that spring of 1984, I spent at least three days a week on the movie set. I was able to arrange for several of my other friends to come on as extras and make a little money as well. In one scene, we all wore Klan robes with all the regalia. I was chosen to do what they call a "head shot" … a shot where my face filled the entire screen. I was holding a rifle and wearing Klan robes with a pair of mirrored Ray Ban's to go with the menacing look on my face. Later that night, we lit a cross while standing in a circle yelling, "White power!".

The next day, a crew member found a business card on the door of the production office in the motel. On the card was a picture of a robed and hooded Klansman riding a robed and hooded horse. The card read, "The Royal Knights of the Ku Klux Klan are watching you". Apparently, we must have done things correctly, because nothing was ever heard from them again.

I had the opportunity to meet all the actors in the movie and spend time with them between shots. Ed Harris and his wife Amy were both down-to-earth people, and I enjoyed every moment I spent with them. They even brought the family dog with them, a beautiful Golden Lab named "Girl", who quickly became a beloved fixture on the set.

I also made friends with several other members of the cast and production crew during that spring. Some of those who liked to get high needed a local drug connection, and naturally, me being me, I was able to be that connection. I spent a lot of days with them hiding behind a production trailer, smoking joints and doing lines of cocaine with some of my new movie friends and customers. I suspect that may have been one of the reasons I had so many days "on call".

When shooting finally came to an end, the producers held a wrap party in the same western honky tonk where the well-known country band "Asleep at the Wheel" had appeared in one of the scenes. The wrap party was a fun night of free drinks and sumptuous food catered by the producers, while I catered an ample supply of high-grade marijuana and cocaine, and partied with just about every one of the major actors and all the crew.

Prior to release of the movie in 1985, I received a letter from the producers asking me to come to Hollywood to participate in a panel that would answer questions just before the showing of the movie. I called them back and told them that I wanted to bring my wife with me as well, but that I couldn't afford to pay a babysitter while we were gone. They told me that I could bring my wife and that they would pay for everything.

Naturally, we agreed to go. A few days later, a limo pulled up to our house in Ingleside and drove us to the airport in Corpus Christi. After arriving in LA, we were driven to the Marriott Sunset Strip. That night, we were driven to the movie premier, where we had the pleasure of renewing our acquaintances with many of the cast members.

One of the commentators on the panel session was Maria Shriver. At the time, she was working for CBS and did an interview with me about the movie and happenings on the Gulf Coast of Texas during those times of unrest between the Vietnamese and local shrimpers.

It had been great fun being a part of that world for a time, especially since my love for movies had been such a big part, and maybe even a driver of my life. The next day, we flew back to Texas, and that was the end of my brief brush with fame.

Since movies have always been so important to me, mainly for their ability to help me escape, I believe that this is a good place to end this story. My life, of course, has gone on for another forty-odd years, and much has happened in that time, but this was meant to be a finite story. A story about my time growing up in Texas and how that helped shape me into the person I became. It's the story of a bandit. A social bandit who tried so hard to live a conventional life. A conventional life that had somehow always managed to elude me until I gathered the courage to rid myself of the disease of drug addiction.

EPILOGUE

I spent the years 1985 through 1988 working with my brother on dredge boats on the island of Antiqua in the West Indies and in Louisiana. By the fall of 1988, my marriage to Michelle was just about finished. I missed my daughters and found out that most of the money I had been sending home had been spent on drugs. We later divorced.

In December of 1988, my father wrote goodbye to me and my brother on a little chalkboard while he was on a ventilator in ICU. He died shortly thereafter. Despite all the things I had done, he had never let me down.

After trying to start a lawn service, I landed a job as the engineer on an exact replica of the English galleon, the Golden Hinde, the ship Sir Francis Drake used to circumnavigate the globe in 1577. The ship was a living museum and we traveled from port to port along the Gulf Coast until I left the boat in 1989 to take a job as a bartender in Port Aransas.

It was there that I met and married my fourth wife, Pat. She eventually became part owner of the bar while we were married, but struggled with her own demons when it came to alcohol. We drifted apart after three years but remain friends and are still in touch with each other to this day.

I was a good bartender with many steady customers, but I was also still involved with some people in the marijuana and cocaine business and supplemented my income through my association with them. I also began to drink more and began snorting cocaine regularly. My downfall came when I was introduced to crack cocaine, and on February 28, 1997, I finally hit bottom and decided to get clean.

The next day, I entered a drug and alcohol rehabilitation center in Corpus Christi and found a new way to live through Narcotics Anonymous. Today, I have 25 years clean. Eventually, I began working at the same rehab center in December of 1997, where I became a licensed chemical dependency counselor through the Texas State Department of Health. I worked there until I retired in June of 2021, and I am proud to say that over the course of my drug counseling career, I have been able to help thousands of addicts find a new way to live.

In 1996, my brother passed away from a massive heart attack. My mother passed away in 2004, and I had the honor of taking care of her for the last seven-and-a-half years of her life. My stepdaughter, Amanda, died from an overdose in 2007, and Michelle, the mother of my children, passed away in 2018 after being struck by an automobile in a crosswalk. Once I realized she was an addict like me, it was easy to see past my own selfish hurt and I was finally able to forgive her for some of her actions.

I have lost both parents, my only brother, the mother of my children, a daughter, and a man I considered to be just as much of a brother as my real brother. I have seen many of my old Bandido brothers pass on, have been to funerals of some of my former drug smuggling associates, and have attended many more funerals of people who, for one reason or another, never received the message of recovery.

Today, with 25 years clean, I live with my daughter Ashley and eleven-year-old grandson in Oklahoma. I still ride my Harley Davidson motorcycle, however nowadays it has three wheels instead of two. As an extra bonus to my riding, I now have the opportunity and honor to share my story with people I meet along the way.

I have survived the hurting years, the healing years, the helping years, and a liver transplant. At age 77, I am now looking forward to many more happy years, and maybe even another book. God Bless.

Note from the author

Whether about war or crime, stories like Band of Brothers or Goodfellas both portray groups of men united in a common cause during a single period of their lives. We never see every moment of their lives, because only the moments that made them stand out from the ordinary captured our attention. Their stories are pictures in time, as it were. A snapshot of something that occurred during a finite period of their lives, and that's what this is. Rather than a complete, birth-to-present biography, it is a finite story encapsulated within a finite period of my life.

Made in United States
Orlando, FL
16 April 2023

32149277R00063